THE POLLEN PATH

In the house of life I wander
On the pollen path,
With a god of cloud I wander
To a holy place.
With a god ahead I wander
And a god behind.
In the house of life I wander
On the pollen path.

from THE NIGHT CHANT

A SAND PAINTING FROM THE BLESSING CHANT

The initiate enters on the path of the rainbow at the lower right, passes onto the yellow pollen path between the two mysterious Ethkaynaáshi, the Spirit Bringers, and comes into the white field of ritual ceremony through the Navajo tree of life, the Great Corn Plant. He has to pass through both female and male experience as he does so, the female experience symbolized by the smooth, curved lines of the rainbow (red and blue), and the male by the crooked, dynamic lines of the lightning. Passing out at the top through the corn tassels he comes to the Blue Bird, which signifies blessing and peace, and goes out into the world again on the yellow pollen path at upper right.

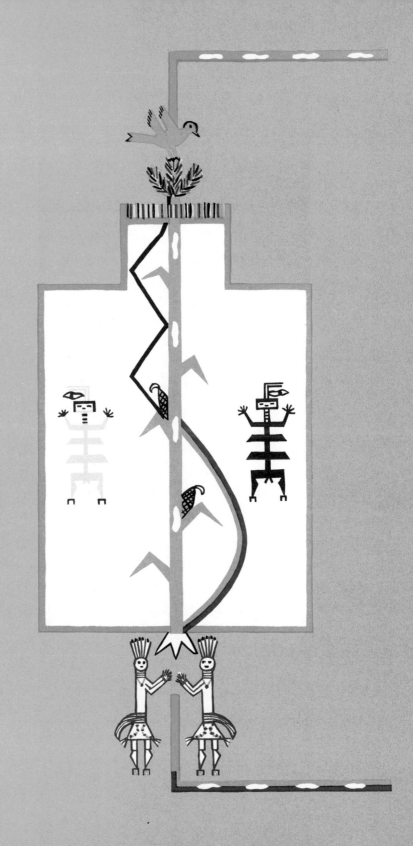

THE POLLEN PATH

A COLLECTION OF NAVAJO MYTHS
RETOLD BY MARGARET SCHEVILL LINK

With a Psychological Commentary by
Joseph L. Henderson, M.D.

■■■■■■■■■■■■■■■■■■■■■■■■■■■

STANFORD UNIVERSITY PRESS: 1956
STANFORD, CALIFORNIA

STANFORD UNIVERSITY PRESS, STANFORD, CALIFORNIA

Published in Great Britain and India by Geoffrey Cumberlege
Oxford University Press, London and Bombay

© 1956 by the Board of Trustees of the Leland Stanford Junior University
Library of Congress Catalog Card Number: 56-7272

Printed and bound in the United States of America by Stanford University Press

Designed by Adrian Wilson

DEDICATED TO THE MEMORY OF
TONI WOLFF

PREFACE

THE FOLLOWING COLLECTION of Navajo stories represents an attempt to delineate and combine in the covers of a readable book the basic myth elements pertaining to the Navajo religion and culture. They are gathered from many sources. Besides my own studies made over a period of twenty-five years, the stories have been told by Colonel Washington Matthews, Mary Cabot Wheelwright, Professor Gladys Reichard, Dr. W. W. Hill, and others. Each published version of these tales may be different, depending on the informant of the individual recorder. Moreover, the interested student must search in a number of libraries, in many government reports, in out-of-print and unobtainable Folk Lore Society publications for the original recording of these stories and legends in order to obtain a comprehensive view of Navajo religious and secular myths. He must try also to find the elusive and fast disappearing Navajo medicine man in order to experience the religious ceremonies themselves.

I have tried to include in this volume as large and as catholic a collection of the essential myths as was possible. They are retold and remolded in some instances, for the sake of a clearer outline, and in order to appeal to the general American reader who does not have access to the innumerable sources. The larger part of the tales is taken from the ritual ceremonies, or chantways, given in the fall of the year for the healing of a patient or patients. These "chants" are great dramatic rituals centered around a myth known to the medicine man or chanter. They include song and dance, prayers to the "far supernatural ones," healing measures such as sweat-bathing, massaging, inhaling of medicinal herbs, the making of sand paintings, and many other forms of healing. We have heard that in the heyday of the religion of The People, or The Dinnéh, as the Navajos call themselves, there were over thirty or these chantways. Today, if anyone wants to see the remnants of two or three of them, he will have to go to the Navajo Reservation soon, for they are disappearing fast. In my book, *Beautiful on the Earth*, I have tried to describe some of the ceremonies I have seen.

My main sources of contact with the Navajos were made through Laura Adams Armer and Lorenzo Hubbell of Oraibi. Laura and Sidney Armer shared their friendship of Lorenzo with me, and together Lorenzo took us to a number of ceremonies given by the Navajos of the western part of the reservation. Lorenzo of Oraibi, trader to the Navajos and Hopis, was nurse, philanthropist and historian of their tribes. During his last illness he asked some of the old men who were storytellers to come to sit beside him. In the autumn of 1943 they told us stories in the long afternoons while I sat and knitted, and Lorenzo interpreted for me.

The myths are frame-tales, notably the Creation Myth. Like the device of Chaucer in *The Canterbury Tales*, the myth holds all the parts of the long rites together and, indeed, all the participants. Like the beads on a rosary, the medicine man tells it over to himself and to his patient, coming now to a song or prayer, now to a medicine brewing or to a sand painting. The story concerns, in the majority of cases, the journey of a hero to the world of the gods. On this journey he goes through many tests, often in the underworld, gains knowledge valuable to his people and brings his experience back to his own world in order to help them.

The pollen path is the way between gods and men and it expresses the harmony that should exist between them. Navajos believe that if a man can place himself on this path he cannot be diseased, and if he is diseased he may have recourse to the medicine man whose ceremonial restores him to the path as a way of healing.

In his commentary Dr. Henderson has demonstrated the modern parallel of this way of healing in the method of psychotherapy developed by C. G. Jung. But it is chiefly as a method of interpreting mythology that this commentary is recommended. It should appeal to everyone interested in bridging the perennial split between anthropology and psychology. The Jungian psychologist does not confuse the content of primitive myths with the content of modern psychopathology. It would, for instance, be all too easy for the modern psychologist to interpret the sexual elements of the coyote stories as an example of the effect of repression at an infantile level, such as we see in the dreams of modern neurotic individuals. The coyote stories are connected with the religious rites in the evil or "not-good" aspect of these chantways. There are, however, many coyote stories which are secular in character, and these may be told at any time of the year. But the sexuality in these stories is itself mythological and therefore not a substitute for reality. To think so would, from the Navajo point of view, indeed be putting the cart before the burro. Instead of moving into the foreground of modern consciousness these stories need a method of interpretation which takes us back in the opposite direction, into the past of "no-time and no-history," as my friend E. E. Cummings would say. As Jung has so often described in his writings, the facts of primitive psychology can only be understood as forming part of an "archetypal" level of awareness.

I am indebted to Professor Jung for his interest in my study of the Navajos, and to the C. G. Jung Institute of Zurich for the opportunity to present my material in a seminar. Dr. Henderson and I are jointly indebted to our late friend and teacher, Fraulein Toni Wolff of Zurich. Her encouragement and criticisms were all the more valuable because of her devotion to the principle of psychological knowledge and self-realization to which she had so long devoted herself as one of the leading members of the Jungian School of Analytical Psychology. The Navajos would have called her the best medicine woman on the reservation. To her sustaining memory we dedicate this book.

In the matter of spelling of Navajo names I have tried to simplify the spelling as much as possible for the general reader. This hypothetical reader is no more interested than the ordinary Navajo in a phonetic spelling. If the Navajo ever adopts an alphabet it will probably be an English one. It is true there are no English equivalents for various gutteral and labial sounds with Navajo pauses before and aft. But we have to do the best we can without complicating the matter further. In other books on Navajo subjects a variety of spellings will be found, some simplified and others rendered in such difficult phonetic symbols as would cause the making of special type for their reproduction. The student has the work in phonetics of Father Berard Haile and of Edward Sapir to which to refer.

In the chapter on Navajo mythology in my former book, *Beautiful on the Earth*, I told the stories of eight of these myths. I have enlarged these and added four other stories, including the Coyote material. The motifs at the chapter headings have been made by myself, as well as the frontispiece, but they are to be taken as general decoration and not in any way as pertaining to the meaning of the particular story. I am indebted to Andrew Tsihnahjinnie for the black-and-white illustrations. This young Navajo, who went from the Navajo reservation to fight for the United States on the beaches of Pacific islands, has come back to Arizona to live between two civilizations. His art work is the reconciling factor.

MARGARET SCHEVILL LINK

TUCSON, ARIZONA
January 1956

CONTENTS

GODS OF THE NAVAJO DRAMA

Estsánatlehi   *The Turquoise Goddess and Changing Woman*

Yolkáiestsan   *The White Shell Woman, Her Sister*

Nayenezgáni   *The Young Warrior God and Slayer of Enemy Monsters, the Son of Estsánatlehi*

Tobadsistsíni   *His Brother*

Hastyéyalti   *The Talking God and Maternal Elder of the Gods*

Hastyéhogan   *The Home God*

Hastyésini   *The God of Fire*

Begóchiddi   *The Yellow-haired God*

Tonénili   *The Water Bearer*

Tsóhanoai   *The Sun Bearer*

Kléhanoai   *The Moon Bearer*

Natséelit   *The Rainbow Goddess*

Ganáskidi   *The Harvest God or Mountain Sheep God*

Tsahadólza   *The Fringed-mouth God*

Hadastsísi   *The Whipping God*

Hastyéeltsi   *The God of Racing*

Hastyéoltoi   *The Goddess of Hunting*

Nastséestsan   *The Spider Woman*

Klíshtso   *The Great Snake*

Níltsi   *The Wind God*

Tóntso   *The Messenger of the Gods*

Tiehóltsodi   *The Water Monster*

Coyote

And many animal and bird gods

THE POLLEN PATH

THE FIRST WORLDS AND THE FLOOD

IN THE BEGINNING there was water everywhere and darkness everywhere. A long time went by. Then from the moving, changing waters, the first world appeared, and from the center of it water flowed out in four directions, to the east and south, to the west and north. Twelve insect beings were the first to live in that world, and there were four monsters which lived in the four oceans which surrounded the flat land. After a while a faint light began to show in the east, and they called it dawn. When blue rose up in the south they called it day, and they began to move around with the changing light. Then yellow light came in the west, and they called it evening. And after that darkness again settled down from the north, and it was night, and they lay down and slept. And the color of the first world was red.

The Insect People were ants and beetles and locusts and dragonflies. There were red, grey, white and black ants. There were yellow, red and black beetles. There were locusts of several kinds, and there were bats, also. At first there was only one word in the first world, and it was the word for peacefulness.

But after a while the Insect People began to quarrel among themselves. The males began to practice witchcraft, and the females began to behave in a strange way. It was said that they allowed the males of other peoples to lie with them at night. In order to settle their quarrels they appealed to Water Monster in the eastern ocean to judge between them, and Water Monster said that they should leave that land and fly to another one above them.

So all the Insect People began to fly around in great circles and swarms, and then they spiraled upward to the sky of the first world, looking for a place to fly through it to the upper land. They flew around it a long time before they found a small opening to the east. It was as narrow and crooked as the tendril of a vine, but they managed to crawl through this opening and found themselves on the muddy surface of the second world.

This was the home of the Swallow People, and the color of it was blue. There were little, round, rough houses with holes at the top scattered over the land, but the Insect People did not see any other people like themselves. They decided to send out locust messengers in each of the four directions. When the locusts returned they said that they had been to the four edges of the world. They had looked over into an abyss of darkness so deep that it had no bottom. But they had seen no other peoples and no food supplies of any kind. The new land was a wide, barren plain with no trees and no stones, no mountains and no grass. There was nothing but brown, muddy earth.

After watching the Swallow People flying in and out of their little mud houses the Insect People held a council and decided to approach them. Since they had wings, feet, legs and heads just as they themselves had, they thought they might be friends, and, when the Swallow People spoke to them, they could understand their language. They began to call each other by the names of kinship, and soon they were all living together in a friendly way. But on the night of the twenty-fourth day the chief of the Swallow People found one of the newcomers sleeping beside his wife, so he called them all together and said that they must leave the new world.

"That is not the way to thank us for letting you live among us," he said. "Be gone from our land, for we do not wish you to live with us any longer."

So the Locust People took the lead and began to fly up again in great circles. They all flew together in a soaring spiral until they touched the sky, but they could not find any opening through which they could fly. The sky was smooth and very hard, and they flew around and around it. While they were circling it they saw the track of a little wind, and, following this, they found a slit in the southern part of the sky. Through this they pushed upward with difficulty, and so came to the third world. And the color of the third world was yellow.

It was the land of the Grasshopper People, and there was a stream flowing through this land. The banks of the stream were full of holes and caves where the people of the third world lived. They sent out the locust messengers to look over the new land, but the Grasshopper People said that that was not necessary—that the land was a bare land with no other people living in it. So they decided to live together with the grasshoppers in the new world, and soon they were all calling each other by their family names. All went well as before until the coming of the twenty-fourth evening. Then the Grasshopper Chief found that he was being treated in the same way that the Swallow Chief had been treated, and he was very angry. He said that he would share his land and his food with the new people, but he did not want to share his wives. He called everyone together and said,

"Be gone from our land! You shall breathe no more of our air, nor eat any more of our food. We cannot trust you, so fly away from here."

So up The People had to fly again, and they flew and they flew in widening circles up to the sky. Some of the Grasshopper People flew with them, and that is the reason why we have grasshoppers with us in the world today. They flew all day in a great spiral, but they could find no opening in the hard, dark sky. They had almost given up hope of getting through to another world when they saw the head of a bird sticking through the western sky. They flew to this place and made their way through the hole onto the surface of the fourth world. And the color of the fourth world was half black and half white.

The People were surprised when they came to the surface of the new world to see four great mountains. They stood in the four

» *The four sacred mountains*

directions and their tops were covered with snow. They sent out the locust messengers to the eastern mountain, but they returned saying that they had found no track or trail of life. Then they sent two messengers to the southern mountain, and they returned saying that they had seen the tracks of two strange animals, the turkey and the deer. The two messengers who went to the western mountain saw no living creature of any kind. But the two who went to the northern mountain said they found a race of strange beings called the Kisáni. This was a race of men who lived in holes in the ground and grew their plants in carefully prepared ground. They cut their hair just above their eyebrows and wore garments of unusual texture. They also acted as friends, for they were willing to share their food with the wanderers. This made The People very happy, and they decided to live in this land with the Kisáni. It seemed to them that the new world was much larger than any of the former worlds.

The next day the Kisáni showed them a stream of water and a raft on which to cross it. The raft was a square one made of four kinds of wood. The log to the east was of white pine, the one to the south of blue spruce, the one to the west of yellow pine, and the one to the north of black spruce. Since the water of the river was red the Kisáni said that they had to use the raft when they came to visit their new friends. After this they showed them their homes and gave them corn and squash from the harvest. The People decided that they would do nothing in the new land which would make the Kisáni unfriendly.

In the late autumn The People heard someone calling from the eastern mountain. The voice sounded away off in the distance, and then it came nearer and nearer. At last they heard a number of voices close at hand. A moment later four strange, very tall beings appeared before them. This was the first time The People saw the Yei, the far, mysterious gods. There was a long white body on the first being which was like the body of Talking God today. There was a long blue body like the body of Water Bearer, a long yellow body like that of the Home God, and a black body

» *The birth of First Man and First Woman*

like that of the Fire God, as they appear today. These strange beings made gestures and movements before The People for four days. They were trying to teach The People to be more like themselves, the Holy Ones. When they left on the fifth day Black Body stayed behind to interpret the signs. He said the Holy Ones wanted The People to become human. There were to be many people, and they wanted the new creatures to have hands and feet instead of the claws of insects. They wanted a different kind of smell to come from them, too. Black Body told them all to go and bathe themselves. The Holy Ones would return in twelve days.

After The People had washed themselves with yucca suds and dried themselves with corn meal they heard the call of The Gods again. Four times they heard it coming nearer and nearer, and closer and clearer. Then the Holy Ones were there. Blue Body and Black Body carried buckskins, and White Body and Yellow Body carried ears of corn. They laid a new white buckskin on the ground and on it placed two ears of corn, a perfect ear of white corn and a perfect ear of yellow corn, with their tips to the east. Under the white ear they placed a white eagle feather and under the yellow corn they placed a yellow feather. Then they placed another buckskin over the ears of corn, and they told everybody to stand to one side. They said the Holy Winds were coming and must have room to enter the place. The White Wind came blowing from the east and the Yellow Wind from the west. They went blowing, blowing, between the skins. And eight stranger people came who were called the Mirage People. While the winds were blowing these people walked four times around and around the skins. And soon the edges of the skins began to move. The tips of the feathers began to stir. When the buckskin was lifted the ears of corn had disappeared, and a man and a woman lay there together. The white ear had become a man, and the yellow a woman.

It was the Holy Winds which gave them life. It is the wind which gives us life. The wind goes into our bodies and comes out of our mouths, and so we live. When the Holy Wind ceases to blow through us it is then that we die. In the skin at the tips of our fingers we can see the trail of the Spirit Wind. It shows us how the winds first blew when our ancestors were born.

So First Woman and First Man were born. The Holy People made a brushwood house for them and led them into it. The far, mysterious ones went before them and said, "Live together now as husband and wife." At the end of four days twins were born to First Man and First Woman. They were both male and female, and they were called the changing ones. At the end of eight days another pair of twins were born, and these were a girl and a boy. It is said that they grew up in four days and lived together as husband and wife. At this time First Man and First Woman had four sets of twins and the first changing ones. Four days after the last twins were born The People heard the call of the Holy Ones again. They came nearer and nearer, and when they arrived, they told First Man and First Woman to prepare for a journey. The Gods took them and all their children with them to their home near the eastern mountain. Here the Holy Ones taught First Man and First Woman all the mysteries. They taught them how to make the masks of the gods in a way that would make certain their presence. They taught them how to sing the sacred songs to make the rain come and the crops grow. The songs were prayers and the prayers were songs, and they learned how to use them in the first ceremony. But it is thought that First Man and First Woman also learned the ways of evil on this journey, for it is the way of witches also to wear masks and to marry those that are too close to them in the ways of kinship.

On their return from the eastern mountain the brothers and sisters left each other. The brothers married into the Mirage Clan and the sisters into the Water Clan. But they kept secret all the mysteries which they had learned when they were with the Holy Ones. The women bore children every four days, and the children grew up in four days. Then they were married and brought other children into the new world. They also married among the Kisáni, or Pueblo People, and they mated also with those who had come from the lower worlds with them. And soon there were people all over the land.

They began to make many farms, and everything was going along in the good way in the fourth world when a strange thing happened. They say that Coyote caused it to happen. Coyote and Badger had been born just after First Man and First Woman had been made, and Coyote was always visiting around and poking his long nose into things around the houses and farms. One day he saw two little girls of The People who were swimming across the river with their mother. Suddenly he saw these two little girls disappear under the waters. Coyote thought that the Water Monster had pulled the girls under the river, and he ran to tell everyone what had happened. The People looked everywhere, but it was not until the Holy Ones came to help them that they knew the little ones were safe in the home of the Water Monster under the waters. He had taken them down there so that they could become playmates for his own two little girls. For three days and three nights The People searched for them. When the fourth morning came they heard the call of the gods coming nearer and nearer, and then White Body and Blue Body appeared carrying large bowls of blue and white shell. Placing these bowls on the surface of the river they caused them to spin around and around, and, gradually, to make a hole down through the water. They told a man and a woman to descend through this passage, and as these two did so, Coyote followed right along behind them. Under the waters they found a large and beautiful house of four rooms. The room in the east was made of dark whirling waters, the room in the south of very blue, shining waters, that in the west of yellow sunset waters, and that in the north of all kinds of colored waters, changing and mixing together. This was the home of Tiehóltsodi, the ruler of the waters.

The man and woman of The People went through the rooms looking for the two little girls. Coyote followed right behind them because he wanted to see how things were for himself. He followed them into the eastern room, but there was no one there. He followed them into the southern and western rooms, but they were empty. Finally in the northern room they all saw the Water Monster sitting playing with his own two little daughters and the little girls of The People. The man and woman seized the two little girls and went back with them to the upper world. While they were doing this Coyote picked up the two little water babies and hid them under his fur robe. Since he never took this robe off, even when he was sleeping, no one noticed anything as he came out of the waters. He was always skulking around anyway, so no one paid any attention to him.

But the next morning very strange things began to take place. The People were frightened to see the sky dark with all kinds of birds and squirrels flying and leaping into the camps. Also they saw herds of deer and antelope streaming past from east to west. For three days there were flocks of turkeys and hawks and hummingbirds and bats flying over the farms. When the morning of the fourth day came The People saw a gleaming white line on the eastern horizon, and they sent out messengers to see what the nature of this thing was. When they found that it was a flood of white foaming water approaching them they did not know what to do. There was water everywhere, the messengers said, water which was very deep and moving along very fast. The People felt helpless and could not decide what to do. The Kisáni joined them, and they wept and moaned together all through the night.

When the dawn light came in the east they saw that the waters were high as mountains and encircling the whole horizon. The People packed up all their hard goods and all their soft goods and climbed to the top of the highest mountain. But as they climbed, the waters whirled around the base of the mountain and rose higher and higher. Then it was that two of the Squirrel People planted the seeds of a juniper and a pinyon tree, and The People had hope as they saw two tall trees grow higher and higher. But after a time the trees began to branch out and to stop growing. Then two of the Weasel People began to plant a pine and a spruce tree, and The People again hoped as they saw these trees grow faster and faster into the sky. But soon these trees also began to branch out and to grow to small points at their tops, and then The People lost all hope. Just at this moment of their greatest need, as the waters were surging higher and higher, two men were seen walking up the side of the mountain. One was older than the other for he had grey hair. The younger man walked in front of the older man, and as they ascended the mountain The People watched, but no one said a word. The two men sat down on the summit of the mountain, facing the east. The younger man told The People to move away and not to watch what his father and he were doing. From under his shirt the old man took out many little buckskin bags which contained earth from all the mountains of the fourth world. He spread this earth into a mound and planted thirty-two seeds in it. When The People were told to return they saw the roots of little reeds growing down into the earth of the mountain, and soon all the roots joined together and became a great reed which swayed gently as it grew toward the sky. There was a hole in its eastern side, and as the reed grew and grew, The People crowded into this entrance. When they were all safely inside the hole was closed, and it was just in time. Coyote was the first one inside the reed and Turkey was the last one to enter. His tail feathers were caught in the foam on the rising waters, and they have remained white even to this day, and the voice of the surging and foaming waters seemed to say, "Yin, Yin, Yin, Yin."

As the reed grew toward the sky it began to sway back and forth and The People were afraid. But Black Body drew a deep breath which he blew into a thick, dark cloud at the top of the reed, and this held it steady. When the reed touched the sky they sent out the great hawk to see if he could find a hole in the sky. He scratched and scratched with his claws, and finally disappeared from their sight. When he returned he told them that he had seen a faint light, but he had not been able to fly through to it. Then they sent out the locust messenger, and when he returned he told them he had come out on a little island in the midst of a lake. He had seen four large white birds which were either cranes or swans, and they had challenged his right to be in the new world. By this time First Man had called on all of the digging animals to make a larger hole in the sky. The trail of the locust was too small for all The People. So Lynx, Bear, Badger and Coyote clawed their way through and made a good path. Badger got his feet stuck in the black mud, and that is the reason his feet are black to this day.

First Man and First Woman led the way out of the reed onto the surface of the new world, which is the present world. It seemed to stretch out into a wide horizontal plane. But they had the earth from the mountains of the fourth world with them, and they determined to make seven mountains in the new world. The Holy Ones had come into the reed with them, and all was beautiful on the earth. They called it the fifth world. They said that there were four worlds below, and so there must be four worlds above. And the color of the fifth world was white.

THE RIVER OF
SEPARATION

BEFORE The People settled down in the new world they came to the Separation River. First Man and First Woman were leading them, and they decided to make a farm on the southern bank of the river. They stopped up some of the waters and made them run in little streams over the face of the broad land. They pulled down some cottonwood trees and shaped rough tools to drag the weeds and bushes out of the fields. Then they planted the corn seeds which they had brought with them from a former world. They told the Changing Twins—the barren, elder children of First Man and First Woman—to guard each end of the farm.

Now these two were men-women children, and it was at this time that they made the first baskets. The first hermaphrodite, watching at the end of the farm by the dam, noticed some clay of a different color from the earth of the banks about him. He held some of it in the palm of his hand, and it shaped itself into a little bowl. After this he formed a plate and a dipper and a pipe. At the other end of the farm the second twin observed some reeds growing. He picked them, and began to weave them into a water basket. Together they shaped axes from stones and hoes from the shoulder blades of a deer. They also made stirring sticks and grinding stones, and all of these new things made The People very happy. They traded some of them to the stranger people called the Kisáni, and, in exchange, received seeds of different plants. In this way they planted beans and squash and melons on their farm.

One day when one of the hunters had killed a deer he tried

to make a mask out of its head. He wanted to look like a deer when he was out hunting. Some friends of his came to help him, and they continued this mask making for four days. On the morning of the fifth day The Gods came to assist them. The People heard the Yei shouting in the distance, and then they were there, bringing with them the heads of many deer and antelope. They showed the hunters how to cut out places for their eyes and for breathing holes, and how to fit masks properly. They taught them how to walk like the deer with two sticks for the front legs. They taught them all the mysteries of the hunt and all the necessary prayers to recite to the animals.

After this visit of The Gods the hunters were very successful. They killed many deer, so that the farm had all the meat it needed. Then they began to dress the skins of the animals in order to make clothing from them. The People stopped wandering after this happened.

At this time they named the five mountains which they saw rising from the four world quarters and from the center of the world. First Man was the name giver. There was Dark Horizontal Mountain in the east, and he called it Tsisnad-zíni. They found pieces of white shell and white stone on this mountain, so they called the color of it white. The People had brought some little stone images with them from the lower world, and as they placed them on the mountain top they came to life. They were Rock Crystal Boy and Rock Crystal Girl, and they became the guardians of this eastern mountain. So it is today that The People say each mountain has two forms or parts, its outer shape and its inner spirit.

In the south was Tsot-síl, the Great Mountain. On it they found pieces of turquoise and blue stone, so they called the color of it blue. They put Turquoise Boy and Turquoise Girl there to be its guardians and spirits. Doko-slíd was the name of the western mountain, Cloud Water Mountain, and its color was yellow, and an abalone shell was found upon it. White Corn Boy and Yellow Corn Girl were placed there to take care of it. The northern mountain was called Depént-tsa because sheep with big horns lived all over it. Its color was black, for it had jet and cannel coal on it. Grasshopper Girl and Pollen Boy went there to live. The mountain at the center of the earth they called Tso-líhi, and it was round and covered with jewels of all colors. On each of the mountains they put birds of the color of the mountain, and the birds were happy to be there.

Now First Man had become Chief of all The People because he was a great hunter. He brought his wife, First Woman, so many good things to eat that she became very fat—very fat, indeed. He was hunting all over the mountains and over the four quarters of the earth, and she was staying at home cooking many good things. One day he brought her a big, fat buck. She made him a venison stew out of it, with corn and pumpkins, and they had a very good meal. They were sitting together on the side of the fire, and there was only one word between them. This was the word meaning peacefulness. But after a time First Woman wiped her fingers on her skirt and patted herself between the legs. As she stroked herself she made a remark which made First Man very angry.

She said, "Thanks, my vagina."

First Man asked her to repeat the remark. He was not sure that she had said something like that. He wanted to know why she said that. He said she spoke as though her vagina had killed the deer. Did she not understand that it was he himself, First Man, who had killed it? Why did she not thank him properly? First Woman agreed that he had killed the deer, but she also said he did it because he liked to come home to be with her in that way after he had eaten well. She also added that it was for that same reason that the other men liked to come home to their wives after hunting—and at other times.

First Man was so mad he jumped over the fire. He shouted at First Woman, and they had a good quarrel. He said, "So, the women think they are so important to us. Do you think they could live without the men?"

» *The River of Separation*

First Woman said she thought the women could live without the men, but that she knew the men could not live without the women. She said of course the women did not hunt, but they could live very well on corn and seeds. First Man stayed by himself in an angry silence all the night. But First Woman slept very well. Next morning First Man went out early and called to all the men.

"Come hither, all the men," he shouted. "I wish to speak to all the men, but I do not wish to see any women."

He told the men what his wife had said and what the other women thought about their husbands. He told them also to build a big raft. The men were to cross the Separation River and to make a farm on the northern bank. Then he called for the two barren twins who knew the ways of both men and women. They were to live with the men, and they were to bring the grinding stones and pots and baskets with them.

First Man did not eat or sleep for four days and nights. Then he told the barren twins to bring him some food and some water. Four times he had watched the darkness come down over the earth, and he was still very angry. He said he never again wanted to eat the food prepared by First Woman.

So all the men crossed the River of Separation on the large raft, and they kept the raft on their side of the river. They began to build shelters on the northern bank, and soon they had a new farm all planted. The women lived on the southern bank, and they were very contented at first. Whenever a male baby was born one of the older women would go down to the bank of the river, and call over to the men to come and get it. Then one of the hermaphrodites would steer the raft across to claim the male baby. But after a time no more babies were born, either male or female.

The women went about the old farm singing as they planted the corn. They feasted and told stories and had a good time. Sometimes they went to the bank of the river and called jokes across to the men.

"Don't you miss something?" they asked. "There is something you do not have over there," they said.

» The men and women live on opposite sides of the river

And sometimes some of the young men and women tried to swim across to see each other. But the current of the River of Separation was too strong for them, and they were drowned.

The second year came, and the women could not plant as many fields as the men had, so their harvest was smaller. The third year they had even less to eat, and in the fourth year all the women had to eat was a small gathering of seeds.

During the four years of the separation the men had made larger and larger farms. They had also been very successful in their hunting, and they had made many beautiful garments of the deer and antelope skins. The corn and other crops lay in great piles on the northern bank of the river. In the fourth winter the women were starving, but the men had too much to eat.

Some of the women who were hungry for meat kept trying to swim across the river to their husbands, but the waters were too strong for them. They were swept away and were never seen again. Some of the women died of the starving sickness, too.

About this time First Man began to think. He began to understand that something was wrong, that perhaps the men should not be separated from the women. No children were being born, and many of the old men were dying. One evening the venison stew made by one of the hermaphrodites did not taste as good to him as the kind of stew First Woman used to make. He longed for her in other ways too, so he called a council of the men together. He said he did this because he did not want The People to disappear from the face of the earth. He asked the men how they felt about asking the women to come over to live on the northern bank of the river.

One of the men answered him and said, "I have not been able to eat because I know that my wife is hungry."

Another man said, "We shall perish if we live alone."

The third man said, "Perhaps they have learned their lesson by now."

The fourth man said, "They are very poor. Have they not been punished enough?"

But First Man said, "I do not know whether First Woman is sorry because she said those words which made me angry. Tell her to come to the bank of the river to talk to me."

When First Woman did so he called over to her, asking her if she had learned to live alone. And First Woman answered, "We cannot live without our husbands."

First Man told her that was all right, but never to say what she had said to him again. The men and the women then assembled on the two banks of the river, and the raft was sent back and forth to carry the women to the northern bank. First Man said they had to bathe themselves first and to dry themselves with corn meal. He had them all enclosed in a brushwood circle while they were preparing themselves. The men also bathed and shampooed their heads with suds from the soap root. Then they covered themselves all over with pollen. There was to be no coming together of the men and the women until the fourth night. So after a great feast on the evening of the fourth day, there was much rejoicing in the reunion of the men and the women. But there was sadness, too, for many of the men could not find their women, and some of the young men did not know the strange women and girls.

One man who could not find his wife and daughters found that they had been left behind on the southern bank. He went over to try to search for them, but they were not there. Finally when they came to the edge of the water he called to them to jump in, and he would swim with them. The mother was able to get across, but the two girls were swept down the stream and picked up by the Water Monster, Tiehóltsodi. Coyote was the first person to find out that these girls were safe in the underwater house of the Water God. But what happened after that is told in another tale.

Hereafter when the men and the women crossed the River of Separation they crossed it together. But it was said that the women blamed the men ever after for all the deaths by famine and drowning. Of course, the men, too, blamed First Woman for her terrible words, so she kept her tongue to herself after this and learned a few things from Coyote.

The men said, too, that it was during this time of the separation that the monsters were born. They said the women had tried to have intercourse with themselves and with all kinds of old roots and bones. But the women said the monsters were children of the Sun Father, like the young heroes, and the Sun Father agreed that this was so. How the men behaved during the time of the separation of the sexes is not generally told. The storytellers are generally the descendants of those who lived on the northern bank of the River of Separation.

THE TURQUOISE GODDESS ĀND THE TWIN HEROES

SOME SAY Estsánatlehi was born in the fourth world at the time of the great darkness. They say they saw Father Sky leaning down to Mother Earth and Mother Earth rising up to meet Father Sky. When Salt Woman and First Woman went to the place on a mountain top where this had happened they found a small turquoise figure of a woman. The People were glad to have this little figure, and they took great care of it. From it later came Estsánatlehi, the Changing Woman. They called her also the Turquoise Goddess. She it is who is the greatest of the gods of The People. She changes as the seasons change, being young girl or old woman as it is spring or winter. She became the mother of the two young Warrior Gods, the slayers of all the enemy monsters. However, another story says she had a twin sister, Yolkáiestsan, the White Shell Woman, who was the mother of the younger of the heroes. And this is the way we heard it told.

After The People had been in the fourth world for some time they were threatened by monsters. These monsters, or Enemy Gods, began to pursue and kill many of The People. The Monsters were increasing, and The People were growing fewer and fewer. Finally there were only four people left in all the land. An old father and mother and their son and daughter were hiding and trying to save themselves. One morning as they were out hunting seeds and roots they heard the voice of Talking God from the eastern distance. The call was at first very faint and far away, but after a little time it became louder and louder. When they heard it the fourth time they could also hear the shuffling of his feet on the sandy earth, and then there he was before them. He told them to get the small turquoise figure and bring it in twelve days to the top of the mountain which was in the center of the world.

When they had climbed the mountain by a trail which wound around and around it, they saw a party of the Holy Ones near the summit waiting for them. One of them who stood in the east among the Daylight People held in his hands a small figure of a woman made out of white shell. The Holy Ones took the two little figures and laid them on a sacred buckskin with their heads to the east. They also placed two perfect ears of corn with them, one white and one yellow. Then they covered them with another buckskin and stood in a circle around them on the top of the mountain. There was a little opening in the circle toward the east, and in and out of it Níltsi, the Wind God, danced, blowing life between the two buckskins. The Holy Ones sang many songs, and four times they passed in and out of the circle lifting the upper buckskin as they did so. As they raised it the fourth time they saw that the two little figures and the two ears of corn had become living beings. The two ears of corn had changed into White Corn Boy and Yellow Corn Girl, and the two stone figures had become the Turquoise Woman and the White Shell Woman. When Talking God and Home God and the other Holy Ones had departed from the mountain top they took White Corn Boy and Yellow Corn Girl with them, but the two young sisters stayed on the mountain top alone.

After they had lived there for some time they became very lonely. They asked each other if there were no other living beings like themselves. They said they could see nothing but the warm sky above them, and the water falling down the mountain side. Could they be living beings like themselves? In the morning the Turquoise Woman lay down upon a flat bare rock with her feet to the east. She was glad to feel the rising sun shine down upon her. Her sister, the White Shell Woman, went into the course of the dripping waters, and allowed them to fall upon her. Four days after this the White Shell Woman said to her sister,

"Elder Sister, I feel something moving within me. What can it be?"

And the Turquoise Woman said, "It is a child. It was for this that you lay under the waterfall. I also feel the movement of life within me. It was for this I let the Sun shine upon me."

At the end of four days two baby boys were born, and Talking God and Home God came to help at their birth. They were called Nayenezgáni and Tobadsistsíni. At the end of eight days the boys were fully grown, and the gods showed them how to race around the mountain. One night as they lay down to sleep they heard their mothers whispering. The boys tried to listen but could not catch the meaning of the words. At length they arose and went to their mothers and said,

"Mothers, why do you whisper in the night? Of what do you speak?"

"We speak of nothing you wish to know," said the mothers.

"We wish to know who are our fathers," said the boys.

"The round cactus and the sitting cactus are your fathers," answered the two sisters.

After this Estsánatlehi warned the two boys to stay close to their home. She told them there were enemies all over the lower lands. But the sisters made little bows and arrows for their sons and showed them how to hunt with them. Each day the boys went hunting they ventured a little farther away from their home. They disobeyed their mothers and hunted far to the east and then to the south. After this they hunted to the west and to the north. They saw strange black birds hidden in trees. The birds had thin red heads with no feathers on them. They also saw coyotes skulking around and magpies and crows flying. When they told their mothers of these sights the mothers were very sad. They knew that these creatures were the spies of Yeitso, the Giant Monster, and of all the other monsters. They warned the boys again.

One day when the two boys were out hunting they saw some

smoke coming out of a hole in the ground just ahead of them. When they arrived at this place they saw an old black ladder sticking out of the hole. The ladder had four rungs to it, and stepping down them the boys found themselves in the home of the Spider Woman. She was a very old woman with a sharp chin, but she bade the boys welcome and asked them who they were. They told her all about themselves and their mothers. They said they were trying to find the way to the home of their father. As they ate the food she had prepared for them she told them that their father was the Sun Bearer. She also told them how to journey to his house and what dangers to avoid on the way. She gave them life feathers from the breasts of the Enemy Gods, and she told them songs and prayers to help them on their journey.

Now, as they seemed in the beginning to have one mother, so, the story goes, there was only one father. They were now two strong young men, and they were becoming warriors and hunters. They wanted to make the journey to the home of the Sun, so they prepared themselves as Spider Woman directed them. After they left her house they came to four places of great danger. In a narrow pass there were rocks that rolled toward them and tried to crush them. There were cutting reeds with great blades through which they had to pass. There were forests of cane cactus that tried to tear their bodies as they looked for a path through them. But wherever they went they remembered the words of Spider Woman. She had said to them,

"Remember always to walk in the pollen path of peace and of blessing. Be still within yourselves, and know that the trail is beautiful. Whenever you are in danger walk carefully and quietly. Your feet will be blessed with pollen and your hands will be blessed with pollen. Let your minds and your voices go forward on the pollen path."

So they were able to meet all the tests and dangers, and they made peaceful the ways of their enemies. But near the end of their journey they had to pass through the land of the boiling white sands. There were whole deserts of moving, blinding sands.

The dunes whirled about them, and they were boiling hot like flames from a fire. The voice of the sands called out to them and said,

"Who are you, and whence do you come?"

"We come from the land of The People in the center of the earth. We are the children of the Sun Bearer, and we go to seek the house of our father."

They were asked this question four times, and four times they repeated their words with the prayer of Spider Woman. The sands subsided into quietness, and a voice said,

"Pass on to the house of the father."

After this they came to a sheet of broad water, and beyond it they saw a square house made of turquoise. They crossed the river on a rainbow raft made for them by the Holy Ones. As they came to the door of the square house they found that it was guarded by two crouching bears, one on either side of the entrance. But the two young warriors sprinkled pollen on them and repeated the pollen prayer. The two bears lay down and went to sleep. After they were in the entrance way of the house they saw two large snakes, one guarding the left of the way and one the right. But these were also quieted by the pollen prayer. And a third and a fourth set of guardians, a pair of winds and a pair of lightnings, were also made friendly. When they entered the square turquoise house and looked around, they saw a woman sitting in the east and two handsome young men and women sitting in the northern and southern parts of it. The wife of the Sun Bearer said,

"Who are you? And why do you enter here?"

The two young brothers told her they were seeking their father, the Sun Bearer, so she invited them to come in. Although she was angry she wrapped them up in black clouds and hid them over the doorway, for she had told them that her husband allowed no one to enter his house and that he killed anyone who tried to do so.

After sleeping a while and waiting patiently, late in the afternoon they heard a noise as of a great gourd rattle coming from the west. It was made by Tsóhanoai, the Sun Bearer, as he approached his house. As he entered he took the disk of the sun off his back and hung it on a peg in the western wall of the room. Here it clanged and rattled before it became cool. The boys were peeking out of their cloud wrappings, and they were very glad, indeed, to see their father.

Tsóhanoai had seen their footprints as he entered, and he called out in an angry voice,

"Where are the two who came here today? Why did you let them enter?"

He asked this question three times before his wife answered. The fourth time he asked it his wife replied,

"They are two who say you are their father. Yet you always tell me that you visit no other woman. You say you have no wife but me. Whose sons are these, then?"

And she unwrapped the coverings of cloud, and the boys fell out of them at the feet of their father. He seemed not at all glad to see them, for he seized them and threw them against the wall, hoping to kill them. There were sharp spikes of white rock on the wall, but the boys bounded back from them unhurt. The life feathers which Spider Woman had given them were protecting them all the time. Then the Sun Bearer threw them against each wall of his house in turn. He threw them against spikes of turquoise in the southern wall, against yellow spikes in the western wall and against spikes of black rock in the northern wall. Each time that he saw that the boys were uninjured he paused and said,

"It might indeed be true that you are my children."

But he continued to test them. He put them through very hot fires four times in a sweathouse. But after a time he ordered his daughters to spread sky blankets on the ground so that the boys could be made beautiful as his other children were beautiful. As the boys sat on the blankets the girls bathed them and dried them. Then they pulled on their hair so that it would be longer and heavier. They molded their faces and forms until they shone like sons of the sun. The Sun Bearer invited them into his house again and offered them some of his special tobacco. He took his pipe made of turquoise down from the eastern wall and filled it with a tobacco so strong it killed anyone who smoked it. He lighted this pipe by holding it up to the sun disk on the wall.

As the boys sat down by their father they heard a little voice speaking to them. It came from a small blue caterpillar making a trail toward them of tiny, blue drops of spittle. They were warned by this voice of the power of the tobacco and told to put some of the drops of blue spittle into their cheeks so that they would not be harmed. They did as they were told and then they enjoyed the smoking very much. They passed the pipe back and forth, and they told their father that the tobacco tasted very sweet and cool to them.

When Tsohánoai saw that the smoke did not burn them he was satisfied and said,

"My children, why have you taken this long journey? What is it that you want from me?"

"Our father, in the land where The People live there are many monsters. The People are dying and the monsters and the Enemy Gods are increasing. There is the giant Yeitso, the terrible creature called Teelget, and there are many other enemy monsters. Tell us how to rid our land of these creatures. Give us some of your weapons so that we may slay them. Teach us how to be strong so that we may make the land safe for our people."

But the Sun Bearer did not answer them at once. The monsters were also his children, his sons and his daughters and his grandchildren. At last, however, he made up his mind to help the sons of Turquoise Woman. He took garments made of flint flakes from the wall and gave four of them to each boy. He gave them arrows made of lightning and rainbows on which to travel, and great stone knives and clubs. As the boys put the clothing on, streaks of lightning played about them from all directions. Then the Sun Bearer said farewell to his sons and led them to a sky-hole which was in the center of the sky. Through the opening they could look down and see the land of their people spreading out wide and beautiful under them. But the opening was edged by four smooth and shining cliffs which sloped steeply downward. These cliffs were made of white shell, of turquoise, of abalone shell and of black jet. They might have fallen down and killed themselves, for this was the last test of their father. But the Spirit Wind blew around them and held them up as they stood at the top of the cliffs. Sun Bearer said to them,

"These are the cliffs of peace and of war. On which ones will you descend to the earth?"

And the young warriors, his sons, chose the cliffs of black stone, for they sought war with their enemies. Then the Sun Bearer sent them down to earth on a streak of lightning, and they landed on the top of one of the sacred mountains. After descending the mountain on its southern side they came to a lake with a circle of white sand around it. They were being guided by the voices of four of the Holy Ones which were telling them where to find the Giant Yeitso. They spent the night in a cave where they were instructed in all the ways of their enemy. They learned that he showed himself three times each day on the mountains. The fourth time, toward nightfall, he came down to drink from the lake. As he stooped to drink one arm rested on the mountain top while the other arm rested on the high hills at the other side of the valley. His feet stretched away as far as a man could walk between sunrise and sunset. The Holy Ones said to wait for Yeitso early in the morning.

As the curtains of the dawn parted they heard a noise loud as the noise of the thunder, and they beheld the head of Yeitso peering over the eastern mountain. At noonday they saw his head and shoulders over the southern mountain. In the afternoon they saw his body half reared over a hill in the west. And as darkness came down they saw him descending the northern mountain in order to come to the lake to drink. As Yeitso drank, the water in the lake diminished. And as the water withdrew, the two young warriors lost their courage. They should have caught him just as he was lying down, but the time passed and as he arose he saw their faces mirrored in the waters. He roared out,

"Ho, ho, what a good sight this is! Why have I never seen these two little boys before?"

The younger brother said to the older one, "Throw his words right back at him, and perhaps we shall grow strong again."

So the older brother shouted out, "What great thing is this upon the mountains? Where could we have been hunting that we did not see this big game before?"

Four times they threw these words back and forth. Then Yeitso began to hurl bolts of his great power at them. He hurled four bolts rapidly, but the brothers dodged them by jumping on their rainbows. After this the lightnings descended and hit the monster on his head. He went reeling around while the boys shot the arrows which the Sun Bearer had given them into his body. He fell to the east and south, but then he rose up again. Then he fell to the west and north, and after this he did not move again.

They approached the great body very slowly and with great care, but they saw that Yeitso was really dead. Then they cut off his head and threw it over a hill. They had kept his scalp as a trophy. As they saw the blood flowing forth in a stream so great it broke down the rocky wall of the valley, they heard the voice of the Spirit Wind warning them. It said that if the stream of Yeitso's blood reached the home of any of the enemy monsters they would help him to come to life again. So the elder brother took the big stone knife which his father had given him and made a deep cut in the earth across the path of the river of blood. And the blood filled the hole and then turned into piles of black rock which can be seen to this day.

The two young warriors gathered the broken arrows of Yeitso and took them with his scalp to their home. The mothers were very glad indeed to see their sons for they had been afraid that the two boys had been killed by the enemy monsters. They could not believe that the boys had killed Yeitso until they saw the scalp and arrows. But when the two young warriors wanted to know where Teelget lived the mothers were frightened and wished to protect them from further danger. Nayenezgáni, the elder brother, said that he would go alone to fight Teelget. He told his brother to stay at home in order to make the kethάwns, or ceremonial cigarettes, which were to stand for the necessary sacrifices. He informed the mothers that they had met Talking God on their way home, and he had explained everything which they must do for a ceremony. The Grandfather God had taught them all the songs and prayers and had said that Tobadsistsíni must stay at home to make ready all the necessary things.

Then Nayenezgáni went forth to the very edge of the world to look for the monster Teelget. He was now worthy of his name which meant "Slayer of Enemy Gods." He looked around him in all directions. Behind him was the great horizontal plain of the world. Beyond him there was no world, only an abyss. As he stood looking at the plain, there in the very middle of it was the dark form of a monster lying down. He thought for a long time about how he should approach it without being seen. As he made ready to hurl one of his lightning arrows he heard the voice of Gopher asking him why he had come there. Gopher said that if Nayenezgáni would give him the hide of Teelget he would show him a safe way to kill the monster. When he was promised the hide Gopher just disappeared into a hole in the ground.

Elder Brother watched Teelget for a long time. He saw the great creature rise, and he was like no animal he had ever seen before. He saw the monster shake himself, take little trails in all directions, as if he were keeping watch, then settle down in the middle of the plain. He seemed to be a very large animal with four great feet and the horns of a deer.

When Gopher appeared again he told Elder Brother he had dug a tunnel under Teelget. The tunnel had cross passages at the end so that Elder Brother could hide in various places if he needed to do so. And there was a hole right at the end of the tunnel which lay under Teelget's heart.

Nayenezgáni crawled through the tunnel and looked up through the shaft at the end of it. There he saw the great heart

of Teelget beating and beating. He threw an arrow of lightning
into it, and hid in the eastern part of the tunnel.

Teelget roared and whirled into the air. He ripped up the
ground around him with his horns. The noise of his roaring echoed
all around. As he ripped into the eastern passage Elder Brother
fled into the southern arm of the tunnel. As Teelget tore that open,
too, he fled into the western cross-arm. When that was destroyed,
Elder Brother crawled into the northern passage. And just as he
arrived there Teelget fell down and lay still. Elder Brother did
not know that Teelget was dead till Old Man Ground Squirrel
came and danced on the horns. Then he took one of the paws for
a trophy and gave the rest of the hide to Gopher.

When Nayenezgáni went home he was received with great joy
as his family had begun to fear for him. He showed them the
trophy from the body of Teelget, and they rejoiced that another
of the enemy monsters was slain. He told them that as soon as
he was rested he would go to find the winged pair known as the
Tsenaháli, but his mother begged him to stay at home. She told
him all about the power of the Tsenaháli, how fierce and strong
they were. She said that they had killed great numbers of The
People. But next morning while the family was asleep he rose
and stole away from his home. He climbed a range of mountains
to the west and traveled all day until he came to a place where two
great snakes lay just in front of a cave in a canyon. He was seeking
the knowledge which these snakes could give him, so he walked
slowly along the back of one and then the other. After giving
him their power the two serpents turned slowly to stone. And if
anyone goes to that place today he can see them lying there by
that cave in the mountains.

As Elder Brother was walking along he saw before him a
great black rock. It seemed to be shaped like a bird, and as he
approached it he heard a rushing of wings overhead. It was like
the sound of a whirlwind, and, looking up, he saw the male Tsenaháli ready to strike at him. He barely had time to throw himself
on the earth when the creature swooped past him. Three times

the monster did this, and three times Elder Brother escaped. But the fourth time, as the monster bird flew from the north, Nayenez-gáni did not move quickly enough. The great bird seized him and bore him away to its retreat in the mountains. Here, high among the cliffs where his nest was, the monster dropped the young hero. Although all of his other victims had been killed by this fall Elder Brother was not hurt at all. He was protected by the life feather which Spider Woman had given him, and he repeated the prayer of the pollen path as the male Tsenaháli flew away to tell his mate that the young warrior was dead.

There were two young Tsenaháli in the nest, and they told Nayenezgáni that their parents would return very soon. He placed himself in readiness with his lightning arrows in his hands, and as the male bird approached the nest on the ledge at evening time he slew him with the arrow from his right hand. A few moments later he killed the female bird with the arrow from his left hand. After this he turned the young birds into an eagle and an owl so that they might be useful to his people.

There were many other monsters left, but the most destructive of them were a family of evil creatures called the Bináye Aháni. These monsters had very large eyes, and they killed people just by looking at them. They lived in a large rock house in the northern mountains. After Elder Brother had rested for a while, he took the trail to the north to find these people. Along with his arrows and other weapons he took a bag of salt with him. When he arrived at their house he found that it was in a large rock with a black hole for a doorway. So he walked right in and sat down at the northern side of it. The old father and mother of the Bináye Aháni stared and stared at him with their large glaring eyes. And all the children glared at him, too. Flashes of lightning streamed at him from their eye sockets. But the power of Nayenezgáni was greater than their power, so all of their weapons glanced off his clothing harmlessly. Then they all stared harder and harder at him with their eyes sticking far out from their faces. But nothing happened to the young hero. He just sat there and stared back at them. After a time he threw the bag of salt into the fire at the center of the room. The salt sputtered and flew in all directions. It flew into the eyes of this evil family and made all of them blind. Then Nayenezgáni cut off their heads with his big stone knife.

He had killed the most dangerous of the enemy monsters, so now he thought he would go home to rest. As he walked back over the mountains he met no enemy on his way. Everyone called him by the names of kinship. And his mother and brother were very glad to see him.

THE CHANGING COYOTE

THIS STORY is about Ma-i, the Coyote. It is about his journey on the life way. Sometimes he was a god, sometimes a man, sometimes an animal—sometimes all three at once—and a devil, too. Some of the storytellers say he was there in the first world, in the beginning world with First Woman and First Man. They say that there was a Water Coyote and an Earth Coyote there. Others say that only insects were able to live there in the changing dark waters. They say that Coyote was born in the fourth world after The People had ascended from the third world and had been there eight years. One day some people saw the Sky Father bend down to Earth Mother, covering her in the form of a dark cloud. For a moment they were together, and then there sprang out of the earth Badger and Coyote. Coyote was the elder of the two, and he attached himself to the people of the fourth world and ran around their camps. Badger went right down into the earth again through the passage which led down into the third world.

They say in the beginning Ma-i was just lazy and mischievous. He did not like to work as hard as other people did, so sometimes he had too much time on his hands. He became very restless and always wanted to be going places. He began to play tricks on people and to mislay things. He liked things to keep changing all the time. Although there were two trails of life on which he could move, he began to frequent one of them. These paths ran together side by side in a spiral, and one was yellow and one was white. On the white trail he was known as the good and wise coyote; on the other one, he was evil and treacherous. He could move from one

» *Coyote just traveling along*

trail to the other just as he wished because all things were together in the beginning. He began to like the yellow trail better, however, and so he began to be known as a witch. But he was still Ma-i, the Changing Coyote. And when you see him today and hear him called by his name—the outlaw of the desert—he is both yellow and white, yellow in the upper fur and white on his belly and legs.

But what was there about him which made him seem different? Was it because he could smell things out with his long nose, things about which no one else knew? Anyway, he became impatient and always in a hurry, so people began to avoid him. He also kept his long fur robe wrapped tightly around him, and The People began to think of him as a thief. There was not anything very bad about being a thief in those days, because people thought if you did not take enough care of your hard goods and your soft goods you deserved to lose them. But they wondered what it was he was trying to hide under his robe. He even wore it to bed with him. He had too many secrets, it was said.

After the women and men lived apart on opposite banks of the River of Separation, Coyote was sitting one day on the north bank of the river just looking at the river and sky. He was just doing nothing and enjoying himself. Suddenly he saw the Water Monster come up and steal two little girls of The People. Their mother was trying to swim across the stream to her husband, and she had her two little daughters, one on each side of her. The current was too strong for her and the little girls were swept down the stream by Tiehóltsodi, the Water God.

When Coyote had stolen the Water Monster's children in a former world he had caused the great flood. But now The People were in a new world and wanted no more floods. When they sought some way of knowing their fate in their new home, an old man threw a hide-scraper into the water and said, "If it sinks, we shall all be destroyed. If it floats, we shall live." When it floated, everyone was very glad. But Coyote was not satisfied with this way of doing things. He always thought he knew better than other people. So he pushed himself forward and said, "Let me try it. I can help you to know what is going to happen." So he picked up a stone and threw it into the water and said, "If it sinks, we are going to die. If it floats, we will live forever." When it sank, everyone was very angry at Coyote and cursed him. But he stood up to all the angry ones, and told them that it would be better for them all to take turns dying—because in that way there would be room for the children on the new earth, and for many cornfields. Then everyone became silent, for they knew he was right; but they did not like him any the better for that. And from that day on when they thought of Coyote they thought of death.

On the morning of the fourth day, after The People had emerged from the lower world, one of the twin hermaphrodites noticed water rising up through the Place of Emergence. Being afraid of another flood First Man called a council in order to talk things over. While they were talking Coyote kept skulking around and behaving very strangely. He kept trying to get the attention of the Black God of Fire, who was his companion very often. He kept pointing with his lips stuck out, as people do when they wish to call attention to something. First Man noticed this and said,

"Look at Ma-i over there. He is holding his robe very tightly around him even though it is a warm day. I think he has stolen something and does not want us to know what it is."

So they tore the fur robe off Coyote and were astonished to see the water babies drop out from under his arms. The People put them back in the waters which were welling up higher and higher from the Place of Emergence. They placed sacrifices and peace offerings to the Water Monster with them. They placed a big abalone shell filled with pieces of turquoise and white shell on the horns of Tiehóltsodi which they saw just below the water. But they were also careful to take some of the pollen which had fallen from the bodies of the water babies, for they knew it would bring them rain and clouds and crops. In an instant all the waters were still. Then they rushed down into the lower world with a loud sucking noise.

The man-woman person who had looked down into the lower world died soon after this. That is, he-she ceased to breathe, and everyone wondered what had become of her breath. Coyote took charge of things and laid her body out among the rocks. But The People continued to look for the trail of her breath. Later when her twin looked down into the Place of Emergence she saw this first one sitting in the fourth world combing her hair. But in four days this other twin died, too. So then The People were afraid to look on the dead ones, and in some way they connected this fear with Coyote, too.

When Coyote heard that a woman of the Kisáni had brought a perfect ear of corn with her from the farm in the fourth world, he wanted to get some of the young men together and go to steal the corn from her. There were many angry words about this, but the Kisáni said they would share the corn, so it was broken into halves. These were laid on the ground so that a choice could be made, but Coyote was so impatient he picked up the piece nearer to him and ran away with it. This was the tip with the four perfect kernels at the end, but the Kisáni kept the butt end, and so they have larger and better corn to this day than The People do.

Coyote also made trouble when The People were trying to get more light into the world. They were making a sun and moon and trying to put stars in the sky because there were too many hours of darkness. First Woman and First Man made a round disk out of a clear stone. They set pieces of turquoise around it and twined lightning snakes about its edge to protect it, and they called it the sun. At first they made it with four points, but then they changed it to a round shape. They also made the moon out of a round crystal rock and set it in pieces of white shell with holy water around it. With the help of the east wind they pulled and pushed the sun and moon to the edge of the world. There they appointed two grey-haired old men to be the bearers of the sun and moon, and to carry them over the sky at the right times. These two old men received new names of great power. The Sun Bearer was called Tsóhanoai and the Moon Bearer, Kléhanoai. The People were sorry to see the two old men depart from this world, but First Man said not to grieve, for the two would be seen in the sky world, and all who died would be close to them.

Then the Sun Bearer climbed to the top of the sky and there was much more light. But he stopped there and soon the day grew very bright and hot. The People longed for the night to come, but the Sun Bearer would not come. Then Coyote said,

"The old man who is carrying the sun is lonely. He stops because he has not been paid for his work. He wants a life a day or he will not carry his burden. He will not move down the western sky until someone dies."

Shortly after this an old woman stopped breathing, and her body began to grow cold. As this happened the Sun Bearer began to move again. When the Moon Bearer also stopped that night Coyote said it was for the same reason, that he needed pay too. He would not go on until one of The People came to him. It was just at this time on the fourth day that the second man-woman being died, so the Moon Bearer was satisfied and continued his journey to the west.

There were times, however, when the moon did not shine at night, so First Woman and First Man planned to put some smaller lights into the night sky. They made stars out of shining mica, and First Man drew a star map on the ground just the way he wanted the stars to appear in the heavens. He put a little piece in the north which he said would be the star which would never move, and he placed below it seven greater stars. He put a bright piece in the east, one in the south and another in the west; then he went on to plan some bright figures made of stars. He had three beautiful pieces of red shining stone, and he was just going to place these on the star map when Coyote came traveling along. Coyote seized the three red pieces and said they were his stars. But after trying to fit them into the design on the earth he became very impatient and just scooped up big pieces of shining stone and threw them all over the sky. As he did this he blew a big breath after them, and they stuck right where they were. First Man was very angry at

Ma-i, but Ma-i just laughed and asked him why he took so long to do everything.

About this time Coyote went to the camp of the Chicken Hawk People on a visit. He had heard that they were very good hunters. And, since he was a very good hunter himself, he thought he could show them a trick or two. He also wanted to know if they had any power which he did not have, so he dressed himself up in his best clothes, painted red spots on his face and threw over his shoulder his beaver-skin quiver, filled with his special arrows. He was also looking for a new wife, since the woman of The People with whom he had been living had told him to leave her hogan. She said she did not like his wandering ways. When he arrived at the camp of the Chicken Hawk People he saw two beautiful girls of the Humming Bird People who were visiting there. They were dressed in very unusual clothing with many shining feathers sewed on it. There were also rows of deer-hoof pendants on their skirts and sleeves which rattled gaily when they walked. The men were all out hunting when Coyote arrived so he spent the day telling the girls what a great hunter he was. The girls thought him very handsome and whispered to each other about him. He even told them he was a god of the eastern mountain who had no need to hunt in the ordinary way. He said he was chief of all the animals and all he had to do was to will the death of any one of them. He did not have to waste time the way the other hunters did. He could make the animals appear any place he wanted them, too. After telling these things he went to sleep in a brush shelter to await the coming of the men.

When the hunters came the two girls told them about the visitor. The man laughed and told a boy to go over to spy on Coyote. The boy returned and said a very well-dressed stranger was lying there asleep, and he had a very good bow and quiver of arrows. The chief of the Chicken Hawk People then told the younger of the two girls to wait on Coyote and to stay in the shelter with him. Coyote liked her very much when he waked up. He called her Tsikesasnátlehi because the pendants on her dress rattled as she walked. For a time he was very happy with her in the camp of the Chicken Hawk People. But when he discovered that she was the sister of eleven holy young men he became uneasy. That was a different story. It is a long one, too, so it is told by itself as the story of the woman who turned into a bear.

On an early day of his visit Coyote went out with the hunters to show them what he could do. When the party came to the brow of a high hill he told them to hide behind some rocks and he would drive the deer toward them. He went down into the valley and tied a fagot of cedar bark to his tail. He set this on fire and then ran in a wide circle all around the base of the hill. As the fire spread in the tall grass the antelope and deer and smaller game tried to run up the hill and were quickly killed by the hunters. That night they all returned with much meat, and their praise of the hunting ways of Ma-i, the Coyote, was great indeed.

He helped the hunters many times in this way, but finally he became tired of running around the hill, so he thought he would go over into the next valley to see what kind of people lived there. The men waiting on the top of the hill saw the line of fire and smoke coming toward them as usual, but then it seemed to stop and go back to the place from which it started. However, they shot many deer that day so they did not wonder what had become of Coyote. He had heard that there were a lot of bad people over the next hill, and he wanted to see what they were like. Perhaps they had some power of their own and a different way of doing things. As he was following a trail he saw many birds flying in and out of two big trees ahead of him. A tall spruce and a tall pine were filled with birds making a loud noise. After watching them for some time he decided they were playing a game of some kind. They seemed to be enjoying themselves very much, yet they were pulling their eyes out and throwing them up into the tops of the trees. The birds then sat at the base of the tree and called to their eyes to drop back home again. Each bird seemed to catch his own eyes very skillfully in the eye sockets, and this interested Coyote so much he decided he wanted to play the game too.

The birds did not like the stranger who was watching, so they refused to let him play the game. He asked them three times, and three times they said they would not show him how to play. When he asked the fourth time they flew down and dug his eyes out with sharp pieces of wood. Then Coyote threw his eyes to the top of a tree, as he was told to do, and when he called to his eyes, they dropped right back home again. But the birds were flying around him and telling him to go home, so he did not enjoy himself very much. However, he insisted on playing the game four times. After that the birds gathered in the tree tops to decide what should be done with him. They had heard of a traveling stranger about whom people said bad things, and they thought Coyote might be the one. When he threw his eyes up into the tree again some of the birds caught them and tied the eyes together and hung them on a high branch. Coyote called and called to his eyes to come home again, but they never did. So that is the way Coyote lost his good eyes. Now he was blind and frightened. He pointed his nose at the top of the tree and howled and prayed. Finally a little brown bird was sorry for him and made him a new pair of yellow pine gum eyes. And that is the reason that coyotes have yellow eyes to this day.

It took him a long time to crawl to the camp of the hunters. When he arrived he smelled meat cooking. He was given a piece of antelope liver to cook, but when he held it close to the fire his new eyes began to melt. He tried to cook the meat with his back to the fire and began to act very strangely. When some of the Chicken Hawk People lookeed at him they saw yellow gum running out of the corners of his eyes. They had decided that Coyote was a trickster and they wanted to get rid of him. They led him back to his home and he began to follow the sound of the rattles of his wife's dress when he wanted to know where he was. One day one of the men took her skirt, and shaking it, led the blind coyote to the edge of a steep cliff. Thinking that his wife was there, he went traveling right along, fell over the brink of the canyon and was killed on the sharp rocks below.

But he was not really dead because he knew the way to be born again. He kept his life power in the tip of his tail and the end of his nose, and that was not injured by his fall. Slowly, as he lay in the canyon his strength came back to him and some part of his sight. He began to search for his wife. Before he found her he went through many adventures, and after that, too. He had to die four times and to come back to life four times before she would live with him. Then he made her die four times and come back again four times. He taught her all the evil he knew, and she turned into a bear and killed her brothers. In the end of that story the youngest brother became a hero and brought his ten holy brothers back to life, but they would never have anything to do with Coyote again.

Coyote did not care. He had a number of wives, and he went around visiting them. On his journeys he also visited many animal people. He used to hide outside their camps in order to watch them as they worked and played. He wanted to learn their ways and where they kept their power hidden. He knew that there were many animals who were smarter than he was, and he wanted to know why this was so. One day he went to visit Dasáni, the Porcupine. Dasáni invited him to sit down by the fire and eat some meat he would prepare. Then Porcupine just took a small piece of wood, scratched his nose until the blood ran over the wood, and then cooked it on the fire. When Coyote ate this meat, covered over with some young green herbs, it had a delicious taste, and he wanted more and more of it. But the next day when he invited Porcupine to eat with him he tried to prepare the meat in the same way and the chips of wood just burned up in the fire. Dasáni had to go home hungry, and he did not like it.

On his way home Dasáni met Elk who was just going to swim across a wash. He knew there were some young pine trees on the other side so he asked Elk if he could ride across on his back. Elk said he would take him across riding between his horns. But Dasáni did not like that because he thought Elk might shake him off into the water. He asked Elk if he could crawl into his anus and cross the wash in that way. So Elk agreed and Porcupine smoothed down all his quills and crawled in. But when Dasáni was on the far bank he spread all his quills and would not come out, and in that way he killed Elk.

Just as Dasáni was standing there wishing for a knife to skin Elk along came Coyote. Coyote offered to run a race with Dasáni for the carcass, and he won the race. He took out his knife and began to cut while Porcupine offered to hold the skin for him. When they took out the intestines Porcupine offered to wash them at the stream, but after he had done so he ate them. He told Coyote the Water People had stolen them and washed them away. He tricked Coyote about the stomach the same way, but after a while Coyote turned Porcupine over with his knife and found pieces of the intestines in Porcupine's teeth. So Coyote killed Dasáni the Porcupine. Then he piled up the meat from the carcass of Elk and went off to get some of his children to help him carry it away. Before he went he left his dung beside the pile of meat, so that everyone would know that it was his.

After a while the coyote dung began to talk to the body of Porcupine. Coyote had only smashed Dasáni's head, and Porcupine began to get his life force back as he lay there. Coyote came back and found him alive, so he had to kill him three more times to make him lie still. The fourth time he cut him up into little pieces and threw them in different directions. But each time his own dung betrayed him, and told Porcupine how to be whole again. When Coyote returned with his children Porcupine had piled all the meat in the top of a tree, and that was the way he got the better of Coyote. But the head of Dasáni the Porcupine was flat forever after this time.

Although Coyote was held to be a trickster by many of the animals he was also tricked by them many times. One day he found Beaver asleep by the river and, after he had called to him four times, he picked him up and carried him off on the desert where there was no water. Coyote just left him asleep out there and went traveling along on his own way. When Beaver woke up he was angry and followed Coyote's trail back to the water, but it became very dim. However, one day Beaver found Coyote asleep among some rocks, so he just picked him up and carried him to a sand bar in the river. When Coyote woke up, the waters were swirling all around him and a family of beavers were swimming there and making fun of him. Coyote could find no way out of the water, and he became tired and afraid. There was no food for him to eat, and he was very hungry. The beavers told him to eat grass, but when he did so, he vomited it right up. Finally the beavers took pity on him and carried him over the waters.

Then there was a day when Coyote was very hungry indeed and stole some young green corn out of the patch which belonged to Horned Toad. Horned Toad saw him doing this, and he told Coyote he liked people to ask him for his corn and not to steal it. Coyote just laughed at the little toad, and said he'd like some more corn. Horned Toad cooked some for him three times, but when Coyote asked for corn the fourth time Horned Toad was tired of his begging and refused. Coyote just swallowed Horned Toad, and then walked all around the cornfield telling the birds he met that it was his cornfield. After a while he went to the shelter of Horned Toad and went to sleep. Soon after this Horned Toad got his strength back and began to stir about in Coyote's stomach. Coyote thought the young green corn was giving him a stomach ache. But when Horned Toad made a loud hissing noise inside Coyote he waked up and was frightened. He thought that this was the noise spirits made when someone was going to die. But Horned Toad began to laugh and laugh and to call out to Coyote.

"Where am I, where am I? It is very dark in here," he said.

"Ouch, that's my stomach. Stop hurting me," Coyote called back.

"Now I know you are sorry you ate my young green corn. Where am I now?" sang out Horned Toad, giving Coyote another kick.

"Stop hurting me and come out. The place where you are now is in my bowels," said Coyote.

"Where am I now?" yelled Horned Toad as he kept crawling along.

"Get out of there. That's my windpipe," said Coyote, feeling almost choked.

But by this time Horned Toad was in Coyote's heart, and he just cut a cross on it, and Coyote jumped four times into the air and fell back dead. Then Horned Toad crawled out of the anus of Coyote and went back to work in his field.

Another time Coyote and Skunk were stealing some corn from a man who had a large farm. They stole the corn so often it made the man mad and he made a figure out of a big lump of pitch pine and placed it on the way to the cornfield. Skunk saw it first and called out to it to ask what it was doing in his cornfield. When he had asked the question four times he went up to the dummy and hit it right in the stomach. Of course, he stuck fast to the pitch, and the farmer came along and caught him. He told Skunk he was going to take him home and throw him into a pot of hot water. Skunk didn't want to use his usual weapon because it would only make the man madder, so he stayed quietly where he had been tied to a post while the man went into the house to get some water boiling. Coyote followed the trail of the man and the skunk out of curiosity. When he found Skunk tied outside the man's house he asked how things were with him. Skunk said they were all right, that the man wanted him to marry his daughter, but that he did not know what to do to get married. Coyote said he knew all about that and that he would take Skunk's place. So he untied Skunk and tied himself to the post. The man came out and began to pour boiling water on Coyote, and Coyote howled and howled. The man's wife came out to see what was going on. She was sorry for Coyote and begged the man to let him go. So he promised the man to steal no more of his corn and set off on the trail of Skunk. But for some reason Skunk was hiding somewhere, and he always seemed to be able to get out of Coyote's way after that.

Now Coyote had a great wish. He longed to be able to fly. He used to watch the birds and wonder about the power which kept them up in the air. He would run along the ground and then jump high in the air, but he always fell back on the earth and hurt himself. One day he was lying by a spring under some cottonwood trees watching some larks which were flying above him. They came down on the ground just beyond him and seemed to be picking up seeds. He begged them to teach him to fly. He thought he would like to be a winged being like themselves. The birds laughed at him, and said he would have to learn to pick up seeds first. So he tried and tried to pick up seeds in the way which they did, but he just scratched his long nose on the ground. After he had begged them often enough the birds agreed to pull some feathers out of their wings and to fasten them with grasses to his front legs. Coyote took a great leap into the air, but he fell right back onto the ground. The larks said he should hold his front feet against his chest and take off in that position, but this advice did not help him either. He decided that the birds had lightning power under their wings, and he became very weary of the whole thing. The birds said they would try to lift him off the ground, and they all got under him and lifted him three times. When they did this the fourth time Coyote actually stayed up in the air and began to fly. But when the birds saw him up in the air they were frightened. They thought it could not be right for a land animal to be able to fly. As he followed them across a water hole each bird snatched back the feather he had given Coyote, and so he fell into the water and was drowned.

But he came back to life again, as he always did, and in the evening light beside the water he saw some flickers flying. Under their wings he saw a flash of red light, and he wondered what caused it. He begged the flickers to give him some of the lightning power which they carried under their wings, and after a time, they each gave him a wing feather. Just as he was tying all the red feathers to his front legs a little old grey rock wren came along. She said Coyote had better listen to her, that he was better off on the earth because he was a land animal. Then she scolded the flickers for giving away their feathers. Coyote was very angry at her. He flapped his legs for four nights, but no red light came. So he blamed it all on a little grey bird.

He arrived at his home very cross and tired. He did not like his present wife, and he wondered what he could do about it. She had become a scolder, and she was never just where he wanted her at night. Soon after this he met Wild Cat who was carrying a large bundle on his back. When Coyote asked Wild Cat what was in the bundle, Wild Cat said that it was his wife. Wild Cat said she wanted him to bring so much meat home to her that he was tired of hunting, so he just killed her and tied her up in a bundle. Coyote wanted to know why Wild Cat carried the bundle around all the time. Wild Cat said it was very useful that way. He said that any time he wanted to have intercourse with his wife he knew just where she was. And he also added that if the bundle became too heavy he would just cut out the necessary parts and carry them around with him. Wild Cat was having a good laugh inside himself at the serious way in which Coyote took everything he said. His wife was home in her own hogan, and he was taking some game which he had just caught home to her.

Coyote thought and thought about what Wild Cat had said. Finally he went home to his wife and asked her if it was all right if he went ahead in a new plan which he had. He asked her this question for three days and nights, and on the fourth night she was so tired of hearing him ask the same question that she said she thought it would be all right for him to go ahead. So Coyote took up a big stick and killed her. He wrapped her up in an old hide and began to carry her around with him. But his wife's body became very stiff and hard, and he liked her less than when she had been alive and warm. Also he was not catching any game because of the strong scent, so he gave up the plan which Wild Cat had told him, and went to look for a new wife.

When Coyote was growing older he became very fond of his daughter. She seemed to look like her mother when the mother was younger. He began to desire her in the way in which witches behave toward those who are close to them in the family. It was winter time, and he told many stories to his family as they sat around the fire. He boasted to his wife and son and daughter about what a great hunter he was. He said he was The Coyote, that there was no other coyote like him. After a while he stopped talking and made believe he was very sick. He told his family that he thought he was going to die. He hoped they would miss him as the great hunter of that region. He ordered them to build a shelter and to put his body on top of it. They were to put brush all around it and light fires on the four sides. After they had done this they were to go south to another home, and not to look back toward the fire. He said that as they traveled toward the south they would meet a stranger who would look a little like him. He also said this man would be a good husband for his daughter because he also was a great hunter and would provide them all with food.

Coyote's wife and son and daughter cried when he made choking noises and seemed about to die. But they did all that he had told them to do, and started southward toward the dwellings of the mother's clan. The son, however, did not obey all his father's wishes. He was full of curiosity like his father, and he looked back at the fire. He thought he saw his father jump off the burning brush. When he told this to his mother she scolded him, and said he must not speak of the dead or he would die himself. As they went on through the mountains they became very hungry. One evening they saw a man on the road just ahead of them. The mother hoped that this would be the hunter about whom her husband had spoken, but she did not look right at him because mothers-in-law are not supposed to look at their sons-in-law. She told her daughter to go ahead to meet the stranger while her son and she hid behind a little hill until they could know what had happened.

The girl was young and very shy, but she went to meet the strange man whose face was painted with red spots. He turned his head as he talked to her, and she had hers bowed down most of the time, so she did not get a good look at him. She told him that her father had died, and the stranger said he had known that mighty hunter. He also said Coyote had been a cousin of his and that they used to run and hunt together. He gave the girl some dried meat as a present for her family and told her that he would like to marry her. When she took the meat back to her mother and brother they were very happy to have it, as it was the kind of meat Coyote prepared for them. They said she must go back to the camp of the stranger and prepare his fire and cook for him.

So she went back to him as the curtain of darkness fell and made his fire. Coyote turned his face away from the light of the fire, but when it was dark he lay with the girl all night long. At the first sign of morning light he arose and went away to hunt all day. The girl went back to her mother's camp and told her all that had happened. Her brother was curious about this new husband, so he hid and waited until Coyote came back at nightfall. When he saw that the man was really his father he was very angry and ran back to tell the mother. She would not believe him and still said he must not talk about the dead. But she wondered about some of the things he had said. After three nights had gone by she asked her daughter whether her husband had a mole on the back of his neck. When the girl found this mole in just the place which her mother had spoken of, she was frightened. Her mother knew now that this man was Coyote, and she ran over to his camp and hit him with a burning stick until he ran away. The daughter was ashamed and did not know what to do. They went home to live with her mother's clan. When she found that she was going to have a baby she hid herself in a badger's cave, and left the baby there when it was born. An old owl saw her do this and saved the baby, which afterward grew up to be one of the monsters.

Forever after this Coyote was made fun of as the man who had married his own daughter.

They say there are more stories about Coyote than can ever be told. He was always turning up in unexpected places and doing things that other people did not do. Yet some of The People say good things about him as well as bad things. They say he was supposed to bring fire for the people of the earth to use, and some people say he grew the first tobacco also. These said that one day he took a journey to the house of the Sun Bearer. The Sun Bearer was not at home, but Coyote told his wife that he was a kinsman. She believed him and passed him the Sun Bearer's tobacco pouch so that he could have a smoke. He liked this very much, and when she was not looking he stole a handful of tobacco and escaped with it. The Sun Bearer was mad at his wife when he heard about this visit. He descended to the earth and followed the trail of Coyote by tracing his cigarette ashes. A little rain had covered the trail, and the tobacco had started to grow on the wet earth. First the plants sent out big leaves and then little flowers. After this the seeds of the tobacco ripened quickly, and a wind came and blew them all over the land. And they say it was a very good sight to see. When the Sun Bearer saw how many plants had grown he gave up and went back to his eastern house.

But Coyote just kept traveling along the trail of life. Now you see him, and now he is gone. Perhaps you can catch a glimpse of him in the evening light in the high country looking out at you from behind a bush or group of rocks. If he is a white coyote The People say he will bring you good luck, but if he is a yellow coyote look out—there is some mischief going on. For he is still Ma-i, the Changing Coyote, and he just keeps traveling along.

THE WOMAN WHO
BECAME A BEAR

THE STORY of Tsikesasnátlehi is from the Origin Legend of the Navajos. This maiden is also the Bear Goddess of the Mountain Chant. Her clothes rustle or rattle as she walks because she wears many deer-hoof pendants. So her name really means Maiden-Whose-Clothes-Rattle, who is changing into a bear. Since she is the principal wife of Coyote she is important for a number of reasons.

In the early days the Bear Maiden was famous for her beauty through all the land of The People. She was the only sister of eleven divine brothers, and she had been sought in marriage by the Sun Bearer and many powerful gods. But she had refused them all because they could not pass certain tests which she proposed to them.

Now Coyote heard about this, and, being a vain, good-looking man and very well-dressed, he called himself a god and went to visit Tsikesasnátlehi. In the past he had accomplished many things by his cleverness—by thinking faster than the other men around him. The brothers of Tsikesas tried to destroy him on his first visit, but he did not die because he had hidden his life force in the tip of his tail and the end of his nose. No one expected it to be in these places, so every time he was destroyed he always came back to life.

The first time she saw him the Bear Maiden looked at him with scorn. He was just curious about her at first, but he probably made her wonder about him. She said that he could not meet any of her conditions, and told him to go away. He asked her four times to marry him, and the fourth time she had to take him seriously and

tell him the first condition. She said she would not consider anyone for a husband who had not killed one of the Enemy Gods.
Now Coyote knew one of these—Yelápahi, the Brown Giant—so
he now went to him and killed him in a deceitful way while
Yelápahi was in the sweathouse. Or rather, through his cleverness, he caused the Brown Giant to kill himself. Coyote then took
the scalp to Bear Maiden. He knew she could not mistake it because it was yellow-haired, and only The Gods had yellow hair.
But she said he must do many other things also. He asked her if
she spoke truth four times, and four times she said that she did.
So he gave himself up to her to do with as she wished. She began
to throw rocks at him and finally killed him and covered him up
with stones. But she had not injured the tip of his nose or tail, so
he came alive again. Three times she worked harder and harder
to crush him into little bits, and three times he was reborn. The
fourth time she worked so hard to destroy him that she practically
ground him to powder as she would corn, but she had not hurt the
tip of his tail or his nose. This fourth time, however, it took
Coyote a long time to pull himself together again.

The Bear Maiden was making a basket in her hogan. She was
sure she had rid herself of her unwelcome lover. But back he came,
and she had to accept him. It was after this that she became an evil
person, for she had lain with an evil person. As nightfall approached she warned him of the coming of her brothers. She
showed him where to hide, for she was now all on the side of her
husband, and had forgotten her love for her brothers.

As the pot was boiling over the fire the brothers detected a
strange odor in the hogan. It was a very strong smell. They
thought it must come from the wood of which the fire was made,
so they changed the wood three times. The fourth time the oldest
brother asked his sister what was the matter. At this Coyote jumped
out from his hiding place and announced himself by calling them
his "brothers-in-law." He then left the hogan with the Bear
Maiden. They took all the household goods with them, since all
the pots, skins, baskets and awls belonged to her. Coyote stole a

brand from the fire, and with this he started his own new fire. He then built a shelter around it for his wife.

The oldest brother told the youngest to hide outside the new home and to report on the actions of Coyote. The youngest brother saw their sister put her hand on Coyote's knee. He also saw Coyote thrust it away. Coyote was angry at the Bear Maiden. He said he would have no woman for his wife whom he could not kill four times, so Bear Maiden put herself into his hands and told him to do as he would with her. Bear Maiden had also hidden her vital power, but not in her body, so she came back to life four times also. After the fourth time they lay down on her pile of skins together. The brother heard them talking occasionally, but he was not able to see all that was happening. He reported that all he saw and heard was *tsin-das*—very evil.

Next morning the brothers went hunting, and, after much begging on the part of Coyote, they allowed him to go with them. He was a great help to them because he drove the animals toward them. In this way they killed four mountain sheep. The brothers cut the meat up and put it in a bundle which they made shrink until it was small enough for one person to carry. They ordered Coyote to carry it home to their hogan. They said not to stop in the canyon on the way. But since he always loved to play he stopped to gamble in the canyon with the Otter People, and lost his skin as a result. He taunted the Spider People and the Swallow People, and they all combined against him to destroy him. So he did not return to his wife.

The brothers arrived home, and Coyote was not there. Bear Maiden came to inquire four times where her husband was. Her brothers told her she was well rid of him, that he must have remained in the canyon and been killed. Bear Maiden went back to her own hogan, and the youngest brother again spied on her. After sleeping a while she arose and went to the east of the hogan. Then she circled it to the south, west and north. She pulled out her right eyetooth, broke off a piece of one of her awls and inserted it in the empty place. As she did this she said, "He who shall hereafter

» *Bear Maiden searches for Youngest Brother*

dream of losing a right eyetooth, shall lose a brother." Then she did the same thing to her left eyetooth, after opening her mouth to the four directions. She now had two great tusks coming out of her mouth, as she said, "He who dreams of losing a left eyetooth, shall lose a sister."

Then she made two tusks in her lower jaw in the same way, and said, touching the right lower canine tooth, "He who dreams of losing this tooth shall lose a child," and of the lower left canine, "He who dreams of losing this tooth shall lose a parent."

As she was pulling out her teeth, hair began to grow on her hands. It continued to spread over her arms and body and legs and feet, leaving only her breasts bare. The younger brother ran back to report all this, but when he returned, the hair had grown over her breasts. She was covered with a shaggy coat of hair like a bear. Her ears began to wag, her snout grew longer, and her nails turned into claws as she continued to move around in the four directions in her hogan. The brothers decided that Coyote must have taught her these mysteries. They soon heard the whistling of a bear, and saw a great she-bear disappear on the trail Coyote had taken the day before. At night she came back groaning and covered with wounds. She had been in the canyon all day slaying the enemies of Coyote. All night long she drew arrowheads out of her body and sucked at her wounds. For four days she fought and dispersed the Otter People, the Swallow and Spider People and all those who had harmed her husband. For four nights she healed herself.

During these four days the brothers had remained in their hogan. But now, knowing that trouble was in store for them, they departed, leaving the youngest brother at home to watch. The remaining ones then divided themselves into four different parties, one of which traveled east, another south, another west, and one to the north.

When they had gone, The Gods sent Whirlwind Boy and Knife Boy to help the youngest brother. They dug a hole for him under the center of the hogan, and, leading from this, they dug four tunnels to the east, south, west and north. They put a piece of

» *Youngest Brother shoots the vital organs of Coyote*

gypsum in at each end of the tunnel to let light into it. They gave him two guardians, Níltsi, the Wind, at his right ear, to warn him of danger by day, and Darkness Boy, at his left ear, to warn him by night.

When morning came the Bear Maiden discovered the flight of her brothers. She poured water on the ground to see which way they had gone. When it flowed east, she rushed off in that direction, killed the three brothers she found and rushed home again. In the same way she went south, west and north, and killed all of the ten who had fled. When she poured water on the ground the fifth time in order to find out what had become of her youngest brother, the water sank directly into the ground. She dug around the old hogan and discovered the soft earth in the center. As she came to the pieces of gypsum she saw her youngest brother, and tried to coax him out. But the Wind whispered to the youngest brother to jump out alone, and he did so. Then he walked to the east, and she followed. He looked at her very calmly and sorrowfully and said, "It is I, your youngest brother—don't you know me?"

"Yes, come, my little brother," she said, "let me comb your hair." So the youngest brother sat in the north so that he could watch her shadow, in order to know all that she was doing. As she combed his hair the shadow of her snout grew longer and longer, and he was warned by the Wind that she might bite off his head. Wind also whispered that her vital force was hidden in a squirrel under a bush near by. He rushed to destroy it, but she caused large cactus plants to grow up in his way. He reached the breathing parts first and shot an arrow of chain lightning into them. As the blood flowed from her body the youngest brother said, "Now I shall revive you, but in another way, my sister. You must be of service to your kind and not a thing of evil." He cut off the head and said to it, "When you come to life again, act well, or again I shall slay you." He threw the head at the trunk of a pine tree, and it turned into a she-bear which started to shuffle off to the forest. Presently it stopped, shaded its head with a paw, looked at the man and said,

"You have bidden me to act well—what shall I do if others attack me?"

"Then you may defend yourself. But never begin a quarrel, and always be a friend to the Dinnéh. Go now to dwell in Black Mountain."

Then the youngest brother, who was now a hero, cut off the nipples and said, "Had you belonged to a good woman and not to a bewitched one, it might have been your luck to suckle men. You were of no use to your kind; now I shall make you of use in another form." He threw the nipples up into a pinyon tree which had never borne fruit, and they became the sweet and edible pinenuts which The People eat today.

Then Darkness Boy and Knife Boy helped him to find the bodies of his brothers, and to restore them to life in a ceremony. They built themselves a new hogan because the old one was now a *Tshindi* hogan with a bad smell. And the hero was given the name of Leyananáni, which meant Born-and-Reared-Under-The-Earth.

THE BEGGAR WANDERER

THIS is a story about a boy of the first created people. He was a wanderer, and he possessed no hard goods and no soft goods, but it was said that he was the grandchild of Estsánatlehi, the Changing Woman. In the time after she was the mother of the two young Warrior Gods she became the mother of five daughters. Four of them were born from her body, but one of them was born of her spirit. This last one was called Bead Woman, and she became the mother of the hero of the Bead Chant. Her son was called Beggar Wanderer, or He-Who-Picks-Up-Scraps. He was so poor that he wandered from place to place living on roots and the seeds of wild plants.

One day when He-Who-Picks-Up-Scraps was out hunting he was captured by two of the Pueblo People. They took him home with them to Broad House and made a slave of him. He had to carry wood and haul water all day long for the people at Broad House. He worked so hard he became rough and callused all over, and he was hungry all the time because he only had scraps to eat. He had to poke around in piles of ashes for his food. He was very hungry indeed.

Some time after his capture a young man from Broad House and one from Blue House had gone out to hunt deer. As they were returning at night after an unsuccessful day they saw a large war-eagle soaring in the sky. They watched him become smaller and smaller until he seemed to disappear over a place called Tall Standing Rock. They set up a forked stick by which to sight this spot, and then they hurried home to tell their people of this discovery. Now in those days there were very few eagles in the land, and it was a great wonder to see one. The Pueblo People called a council, and it was decided to send four men to find the place of the eagle's nest. This they did, for they climbed to the summit of a high cliff and looked down upon a ledge below them to see two young eaglets in a big nest. After the council was told about the nest they made plans to get the young birds. It was a very dangerous thing to do. Some of the older men said to send the Navajo beggar down the face of the rock. They said,

"Let He-Who-Picks-Up-Scraps go down the sharp face of the cliff. He is not much use to us. Let us promise him some food, and he will be glad to go down in a basket on a rope. He can then throw the young birds down to us. The men from Broad House can have one of the young eaglets and the men from Blue House can have the other. We can leave the slave in the nest to die."

So they summoned the Navajo beggar and placed before him a large basket of paper bread of all colors and a big bowl of stewed venison and corn. After he had eaten as he had never done before, they told him of their plan for securing the eaglets. They said he could always eat like that if he would go down into the nest. The Navajo boy thought about this plan for a long time. He felt very comfortable inside himself. He thought that life could be sweet to a man who was not always hungry. His Inner Being One did not warn him of any danger. He decided that if he could always eat good food it might be worth swinging in a basket over the face of the cliff. When he told the men of Broad House and Blue House that he would do as they asked, the people of Blue House climbed with him to the top of the cliff. The people of Broad House went down into the bottom of the canyon so that they could catch the fledglings when he threw them down.

As he walked along he heard a gentle voice telling him to go slowly. It was the voice of one of the winds telling him how to behave when he was in the nest. The Spirit Wind had gone to tell the plan of the Pueblo People to Talking God and Home God. They were on their way to help the beggar wanderer. After the boy had been lowered in a big food basket he saw the two young birds in the nest and began to talk to them. He told them he did not intend any harm to them. He found a dead prairie dog and a rabbit which the parent eagles had left for food so he made a little fire against the rocks of the cliff and cooked them. One of the Butterfly People spoke to him and told him he had better go from that place. But Tóntso, the Messenger Fly, was there too, and gave the boy some advice from the Holy Ones. The eagles would not harm him, they said.

When the big eagles flew home early in the morning they found the beggar boy asleep beside their children. They had brought some corn meal in a little food bowl made of white shell. From it he ate and ate, and yet it never grew empty. Then he drank water from a reed which the father eagle had carried under one of his wings, and no matter how thirsty he was it was always full of water. They also brought with them a fawn and a young mountain sheep for food for their children. They thanked the Navajo boy for his care of the young eagles, and they told him that he too was a child of theirs now. They gave him a new name, Kíniki, which meant Eagle Boy. This name sounded also like the call they gave. They were Eagle Gods, and they had great sky power.

The Pueblo People had been very angry because he had not thrown the eaglets down to them as son as he was in the nest. They called and called to him. They used all the names of kinship to him, but it did not do any good. The old men said,

"My son, throw down the little eagles. My child, my grand-child, where are the little eaglets?"

"My elder brother, my younger brother, throw down to us those little eaglets," the young men shouted.

The next day they tried to bribe him to throw the birds down to the waiting people. They wanted to know what took him so long. If he did not want to throw them down he could put them in the basket and send it up to the cliff top. They called to him for three days. They promised him valuable presents of hard goods and soft goods. When he did not answer them they became angry and tried to set the nest on fire. They shot arrows tied to burning cedar bark into the nest, but the nest was not injured. When they did this the two little eagles hopped to the edge of the nest and dropped clouds of little feathers down onto the people below. These feathers had a dust disease attached to them, and they made the Pueblo People sneeze and sneeze and itch all over.

When the morning of the fourth day came the sky was filled with birds, and there was a great sound as of the rushing of many wings. Forty-eight eagles and hawks flew out of the dawn light to save the Navajo boy and the young eagles. They wrapped the boy in a dark rain cloud, and they carried the little birds in baskets of turquoise and white shell. The older eagles supported them on carrying bands of lightning and rainbows, and they all sang as they ascended to the sky world in great circles of flying wings, up, up, in a great spiral.

The Pueblo People knew that some of the Holy Ones must be helping the beggar wanderer, so they went back to Blue House and to Broad House calling out angry words, and scratching themselves.

But when the eagles and hawks had almost touched the sky world they began to grow weary. Their wings had become wet and heavy from the moisture in the cloud wrappings. They were afraid that they might drop the Navajo boy, so they called out to some arrow snakes who lived in the sky above them. The Snake People looked out and said,

"Ho, ho, what is the matter with your feathers? Why do you not use the power in your wings? If you cannot get our grandchild up here, how do you expect us to do it?"

The Eagle People answered and said,

"Yours is a different kind of power, and we need you now. We will give you some of our feathers if you will come to help."

So the Snake People wove themselves together and made a raft of living snakes, and on this they lifted the boy into the upper world above the sky.

Kíniki—as the boy was now called—looked around him and saw four beautiful square houses high up above the clouds. There was a white house in the east, a blue house in the south, a yellow one in the west and a black one in the north. These were the homes of the Hawk and Eagle People, and the evil ones among them lived in the northern house. In the center of this square sky plaza was a deep spring of water. The eagles told Kíniki to stay in the white house of the east. They warned him not to leave it until they returned in the evening. He was watching a war party which was preparing to leave. He saw them put on their feathered coats and pieces of armor and drop down through the clouds on their lightning rafts. He waited for them to come home in the evening, but when they did so, he heard loud wailing, for many of the eagle warriors did not return. He was very curious to find out who were the enemies of the Eagle People.

The next morning after another war party had gone he disobeyed the command put upon him and left the white house. He had not traveled far on the earth when he saw a little spiral of smoke coming out of a hole. He saw a crooked yellow ladder leaning out of it, and climbed down it on four steps. He found himself in the house of Spider Woman and asked her what he should do to find the enemies of the Eagle People. While she fed him she told him who the enemies were and how to conquer them. She asked for four eagle feathers in return for her counsel. But when he returned to his home in the white house the evil birds of the black house were waiting for him, and they sent spirit arrows into him and killed him.

When the eagles and hawks returned that night they were angry at Kíniki. They had to give a curing ceremony to bring him back to life. After transforming themselves into certain Medicine People they used the healing powers of the wolf, the mountain lion, the beaver and the otter. They made a sand painting with these and other animals in them, and this is one of the sand paintings given today in the Bead Chant. But they were very angry at Kíniki for leaving the white house. They had promised Talking God to take care of his grandson. They could only warn him each morning as they went forth to the battle ground, but he kept right on disobeying them in order to follow them. Each night on their return they found him overcome and spiritless. They had to give a ceremony each night in order that life might return to his body. They said to him,

"Why do you try to follow us? We fight such terrible enemies as you have never seen. We can move as fast as the wind, but they can move much faster. It they can kill our warriors what chance does a man of the Earth People have for his life?"

On the morning after the fourth night Kíniki hid behind a little hill and watched the eagle warriors prepare for battle. As they flew out over a sandy plain a whirlwind arose. Great numbers of bushes and tumbleweeds blew up with the wind, and at the same time, from among the sunflowers, great clouds of bees and wasps ascended. The eagle warriors charged at these whirling creatures, and then many dark eagle forms fell back to the earth. The rest of the eagles and hawks flew past Kíniki in a retreat from the battle. The stinging insects and the tumbleweeds had won the battle. Then the wind died down again. The bees and wasps disappeared among the flowers, and the tumbleweeds lay quiet on the sands. Kíniki went slowly down to the battle ground. Then he made a great pile of the tumbleweeds and set fire to them. When the bees and wasps rushed out at him he spat medicine at them, and they flew away. This medicine had been given to him by Spider Woman, and he thought of her as he took four of the great eagle feathers for her.

As he returned to the white house he heard the wailing of many people. They told him that they were mourning for their kinsmen but that they were also weeping for him. They thought that he had been killed by the Stinging Insect People. When they saw him they began to rejoice for they knew that he had conquered their enemies. The chief of the Eagle People told Kíniki he wanted to give him his daughter in marriage. He took him to a beautiful new house with smooth white walls and a large fireplace. There were grinding stones there and new water jars and pots. The chief of the Eagle People called him "son-in-law." He said that everything he possessed could belong to Kíniki if he would only stay among them. But Kíniki wanted to visit the Earth People again.

He thought he would like to see his family before he was married. He told all of his wishes to the Eagle Chief. It was decided that he should go earthward but that before he went he should learn all the songs and sacrifices for a new ceremony. He worked very hard to learn all the new knowledge, and the night before he was to return to his home there was a great feast. All the principal men of the four houses came to visit and to thank him for helping them. Maidens from the white house came bringing a large bowl of white shell. Maidens from the blue house brought soapweed and prepared it with water in the shell bowl. The maidens from the white house then washed his long hair in the foaming white suds. The maidens of the blue house washed his feet and legs, and those from the yellow house dried them with corn meal. When the bath was finished the maidens all went away, but they returned soon with the maidens from the black house. Each maiden carried a bowl filled with a delicious kind of food. And Kíniki ate and ate until he was satisfied. He thought to himself that he had not been hungry in a long time. He smoked some of the eagle tobacco, and then went to sleep on beautiful feather robes and blankets which the maidens had spread for him on the floor.

The next morning the Eagle People put a robe of eagle feathers on him and led him to a sky-hole. They said to him,

"Our younger brother, when you came up from the lower world you were wet and heavy. You had to be lifted by Bird People and by Snake People. But now that you have learned to live with us in the sky world things will be different with you. You will be light and able to fly with your own power."

When Kíniki spread his wings all the Eagle People breathed together and made a powerful wind for him. He glided down on it to the top of a mountain in the Navajo country. He looked all around himself and was glad to see his land. Then he took off his feather robe and hid it.

He was very glad to see his mother and family again, but he did not like the smells in their earth house. His family built a new hogan for him, and also a medicine hogan where he could show the new rite to them. He taught his younger brother all the new songs and how to make the proper sacrifices. He showed him how to make the sand paintings and the prayer-sticks. He bathed him and dried him with yellow corn meal, and then they were ready to give the Bead Chant.

The men of Blue House and of Broad House heard about the new ceremony. They had been ill for some time with a strange disease. They called it the feather disease because many of them had been sore and lame from it after attacking the nest of the eagles. They came to see the new medicine man and asked him to cure them with the new rite. They did not recognize Kíniki because he was strong and well-fed now. He did not look like the beggar wanderer, the Navajo slave whom they had known. He was very handsome in his person, for his form and face had been molded in beauty by the powers of the sky world. When they asked him to give the Bead Chant for them, he told them that he would be the chief of the dancers and that his brother would be the medicine man of the ceremony. Then he ordered them to collect all their beads and valuable jewels, because they would be needed in the rites. He told them to gather beads from as many pueblos as possible. He said that the greater the value of the beads, the stronger the effect of the medicine would be.

So they held the ceremony, and Pueblo People came from all the pueblos bringing their jewels with them. On the evening of the last day they built a large circle of evergreen branches, such as we see today in the ceremony called the Mountain Chant. Many fires were lighted, and there was a large fire in the center of the circle. Kíniki danced in and out of the lights from the fires. He danced covered with many valuable strings of turquoise and white shell beads. He had them around his neck and waist and crossed all over his shoulders and arms. He had told his younger brother what he intended to do, and he had said farewell to him before the last night. As he danced around the central fire he seemed now to be in the east, now in the south, now in the west and north. Now he seemed to be rising with the smoke from the fire, now to be on the ground before them. Now they could see him in the darkness, now in the light. But now he seemed to float upward with the smoke. His feet had left the earth and his head was disappearing in the night above them. It took them a long time to realize that he was ascending to the sky world and taking all their wealth with him. They called and screamed to him to come down. The wealth of all the pueblos was on his body. The louder they shouted, the higher he arose. They saw strings of white lightning come to cross under his feet and rainbow bands support him under his shoulders. They knew that the Holy Ones were helping him into the sky world. For The Gods were lifting him in the way, it is said, that they lift the Earth People to the sky world.

And Kíniki, the Eagle Boy, he who had been the beggar wanderer and Navajo slave, was never seen again on the horizontal earth's surface. Only his brother, the new medicine man of the Bead Chant, knew that his spirit was there near him whenever he gave the new ceremony.

HE=WHO=TEACHES=HIMSELF

THIS MYTH is from the Feather Chant. It is about a hero called Natínesthani who was a great player of games and a gambler. His name means He-Who-Teaches-Himself.

He lived with his grandmother and little niece near the hogan of his mother and brothers, by the mountain surrounded by mountains. He had lost all of his belongings at play. And he had also lost all the wealth of his family—all their hard goods and all their soft goods. Only one necklace of beads was left. His brother hung this up on a wall and swore to kill He-Who-Teaches-Himself if he should gamble with it.

His family was very angry indeed. His little niece came to warn him.

So Natínesthani began to think. He lay down to rest, and he thought about many things. He thought at first he would go away to the east and leave his family and his country forever. But then he remembered he had to hunt for his grandmother and niece. The next day he caught many rabbits and woodrats for them and gave them to his grandmother to cook. His pet turkey followed him all around.

He decided to make a long journey. He went to the banks of the Old Age River and cut down a big tree. He hollowed this out so that he could float down the river in it. He wanted to go to the underground lake which lay below the meeting place of the rivers. He had heard it was where the male and female rivers crossed, and he wished to see what he would find there. But before he could enclose himself in the log he heard the call of Talking God. Four times he heard it growing louder and louder. And then The Gods were there.

Talking God told Natínesthani he would be drowned in the log. If he wanted to go to the meeting place of the waters The Gods would fix a log for him. But first he must go home and bathe himself and make ready for a new ceremony. Talking God said to him,

"Wash your body and your hair well with yucca suds. Clean your house within and without. Have all the ashes taken out, and get the sacred baskets ready. Prepare all the original sacred things. Be ready for The Gods in four days."

He-Who-Teaches-Himself had to steal the beads and the baskets and the buckskins. His little niece helped him to make everything ready. At dawn after the fourth night he heard Talking God calling to him. On a rainbow at the door of the hogan Talking God and Home God stood. And they bade the man come with them.

So he traveled on the holy sun-raft of The Gods to the high places where they lived. They led him into a big rock house which was lined with shining crystal. It was full of Holy People, and light shone from all of them.

When food was offered to him in a small bowl he thought it was a poor offering for a stranger. It was a little earthen bowl, and it held corn meal mush. But as he ate and ate, it kept filling itself up. Although his hunger left him, the little bowl was just as full as before. And it was the same way with a little cup of water. It was just a little clay cup, but it never grew empty.

The Gods examined the sacred things very carefully. The Young Warrior Gods looked at everything he had wrapped in his buckskin bundle. And so did Hastyéoltoi, the Shooting Goddess. Then they all smoked strong tobacco together. Nayenezgáni, the older brother, said to him, smiling,

"I hear you were found crawling into a hole which you burned in a big cottonwood. But you can't go places without the raft of The Gods. You know that now."

He-Who-Teaches-Himself told his story. He said he wanted to go as far as the waters would bear him.

So The Gods said they would prepare a good log for him. They had chosen a blue spruce of great size, and the Lightning People were boring it through for him. Some of the other gods made a window of rock crystal, and they put a white cloud in for bedding. Blue and black clouds were made ready to seal him up when he was inside. The Gods also prepared his pet turkey, but the man did not know of this until later.

They carried the log to the river with ropes of rainbow and lightning. They put a sunbeam at each end of it. The Mountain Sheep Gods used their long wands to guide it, and all the Wind Gods pushed from behind. The Water Bearer, Tonénili, danced and made up a song about the beautiful tree The Gods had prepared for him. When they pushed it into the water the log spun round and round. The Gods had to guide it down stream to make it go in a straight line. But the man inside kept singing and singing. And all of his songs were prayers.

The Pueblo People saw the log floating downstream, and they thought it would make a lot of good wood to burn. They tried to pull it out of the water. The Gods had to send down a great shower of rain. Even so the Pueblo People kept tight told of it. So The Gods sent down great hailstones and lightnings to the right and left. The Gods sent lightnings in all directions, and four times they repeated this action. After they had hidden the log in a very dark cloud, and crossed rainbows over it, and made zigzag lightning play over and under it the Pueblos began to be very frightened. Their chief told them all to go home. He began to think it might be a holy log which The Gods were guiding.

So the log floated safely to a place which was called the Blue Waters. And here Talking God was surprised to see it slowly sink. It seems that Water Monster did this to the log. There were Holy Ones under the water too. And Frog, Big Fish and Otter helped Tiehóltsodi, the Water Monster. They wanted to see the man inside the log.

They pulled him down and took him from the log. They took him to the home of Water Monster, which was a big house with four rooms, one under the other. And each room was of a different color. The topmost room was black, the second blue, the third yellow and the last white. Two of Water Monster's pets with blue horns stood at the doorway of the house and guarded it.

Talking God said that they would have to rescue their grandchild. He sent the Water Bearer to make a path through the water. He smoothed the waters with his blue and black water jars and they opened before him. In the fourth room he found Water Monster, and he said to him,

"I seek my grandchild. He is on a journey."

Water Monster answered, "He is my grandchild too. You cannot have him. Be gone from here."

Then Talking God held a council of The Gods. They knew that they would need more help. Hastyésini, the Black God of Fire, sat with his back to them. He took his fire-drill and built a little fire, and just sat there in a corner beside it. Water Bearer came over to tell him what had happened to the man.

He said, "I fear not the holy ones under the water. We will have our grandchild."

So he went down into the waters with Water Bearer, and demanded that Water Monster give up the man.

Water Monster said, "My power is much greater than yours. We are going to keep the earth man down here."

The Fire God just took out his fire-stick and fire-drill. He steadied the stick between his feet and whirled the drill around four times. From a little smoke a great fire started which burned the house of Water Monster and set the surrounding waters on fire. And Water Monster said,

"Come and take your grandchild. But put out this fire with your power. You are more mighty than I am."

So Fire God made a sign to Water Bearer and told him to use the water in his jars to quench the fire he had made. Tonénili, the Water Bearer, gave his own call. Then he took out the stoppers from his blue and black jars and sprinkled water all over the burning waters. Because the water in his jars was holy water, because it was made of male rain and female rain, of hail and snow, of mountain-spring water and water from the four corners of the world, the fire was gone.

And The Gods took the man. The three of them walked in single file with the man in the middle. Tonénili went first to divide the waters, and Hastyésini guarded the rear. As they rose up they heard a strange sound. It came flop, flopping behind them. Looking around they saw Tsal, the Frog. They heard him say,

"Why do you go so quickly? It is evil to be in such a hurry. Don't you know you must first take away the spell we laid on you? Otherwise you will always have the water sickness. You must learn how to make our prayer-sticks and how to paint them in the right colors. You must teach Earth People always to make a sacrifice to us in their ceremonies." And Frog taught the man all the necessary knowledge.

The Gods put the man back into the log and guided it again down the Old Age River. At the end of the waters under the mountains there was a large whirlpool, or whirling lake. The log whirled round the lake four times, and gradually it approached the center. After this it settled on the south shore, and four of The Gods stood around it. They spoke to their grandchild and said,

"We have taken you where you wished to go. We have shown you the way to a new land beyond the waters. We must now give you a new name. You who have been called He-Who-Teaches-Himself shall now be called He-Who-Floats-Upon-The-Waters. Now go sit yonder and turn your back to us."

He did as he was told, and then he ascended a little hill in the west. He saw the log moving away from him, but he did not see any of the Holy Ones. So he sat down to think. He felt very sad. He told himself that it had been his own wish to come on this journey, that if he had stayed at home he might be dead by this time. Yet the more he thought, the sadder he felt. He just sat down and cried.

Then suddenly he heard a very good sound. It was the gobbling of his pet turkey. He was very glad indeed to see his pet, and they lay down and slept together. The turkey spread one of his wings wide over his master, and they slept very well.

In the morning they hunted for food. Although the mountains around them were very high and sharp they found a sloping place to the west. There was a pass there into a little valley with a stream in it. The man thought it looked like a good place for a farm. He wished he had some seeds to plant. His turkey began running around in a circle to the east and south, and then to the west and north. The man and the turkey met in the middle of the circle, and they jumped around and played together. The man said,

"My pet, look around you. Did you ever see a better place for a beautiful farm? If only we had some seeds!"

The turkey just gobbled and spread out his wings.

Then he ran to the east and dropped down four seeds of the white corn plant. At the southern part he dropped four blue corn grains, at the west four yellow grains, at the north four seeds of the many-colored corn. Then he ran to his master and gave him seeds of squash, melons, beans and tobacco.

"I thank you, my pet," said the man. "Now let us make our planting-sticks and sing over them. We will plant our farm in the right way. No one has ever been on this land before me. I will guard my farm well."

At night he slept on a little hill, so that he could wake sometimes and look about him. By day he circled his field. As he worked in it he met no people, and he saw no trail of life. On the fourth morning he saw the corn sprouting. It was a finger-length above the ground. On the fourth night after his work was done he sat beside his fire, facing the east. He was surprised to see a gleam of light. But when he searched far and wide the next day he could find no trace of any dwelling in the mountains. He told his adventures to his turkey. The turkey said it must have been a glow-worm. But that night the man saw the light again, and he set up a forked stick to sight it by. He searched for four days for the distant light, and for four days he could not find it. On the morning after the fourth night he told his pet that he would go once more toward the distant fire, but that if he did not find it that day he would look no longer. The turkey pouted and pouted at his master, and began to act as if he were very angry.

The next morning as the man searched in the east he saw a shelf of rocks which he had not noticed before. Behind some rocks were two large hogans. He thought that very important people must live there. He was ashamed of his garment of rat skins, his worn grass sandals and his blanket made of bark. He put these up into a juniper tree and stepped forth clad only in his breechcloth and his tobacco pouch. He carried his pipe and his bow and arrows and went slowly toward one of the hogans. As he pushed aside the blanket, in the doorway he saw a beautiful young woman sitting sewing shells and beads on a new white buckskin shirt. He looked at her under his eyebrows, for he was ashamed of his appearance.

"Where are the men?" he asked roughly.

"My father and mother are over there," she said, pointing to the other hogan.

Just then the father walked in carrying the man's discarded clothes. He put the ragged bundle down beside his daughter and told her to spread a blanket for his son-in-law to sit on. The girl only smiled and looked sideways.

Then the old man said that the guest must smoke his tobacco, and he went over to his hogan to fetch it.

But the Spirit Wind whispered to the man that he must not smoke the tobacco of the old one. It said that he who smoked this tobacco never breathed again. When the old man offered him a large pipe he took the pipe and emptied it, saying that he always smoked his own tobacco, that his customs differed from the old man's way of doing things. By this time it was late in the afternoon, and he knew he must start back to his farm. But the old man said,

"Do not leave us. My daughter will spread some skins for you. Sleep here with us tonight, my son-in-law."

The next morning when he awakened, his wife had gone to prepare food for him at the hogan of her mother. She returned with a basket full of mush made of the seeds of wild plants. She also had stewed venison in a large bowl. At the edge of the basket her father had spread poison of great power. The Spirit Wind whispered to the man not to touch the mush, but that the venison was very delicious.

After eating, when the man started to leave, the old man said,

"A man should not leave in the morning after his marriage. He should stay for four nights."

And on the following three mornings the old man tried to poison him, and four times the old one failed.

On the fifth day Natínesthani came again to his farm in the valley and searched everywhere for his pet turkey. He followed its tracks to the top of the eastern mountain, but beyond that he could see nothing. He never saw his turkey again. He just sat down on the mountain top and cried and cried. He called to his pet,

"Would that I had taken you with me! How can I get along without you, my pet? You were the beautiful black rain to me, and the mist and the rainbow. You were the beautiful evening rainbow and the lightning. You were the blue corn and the white corn. You were the beautiful yellow corn and the bean plant. Though you are lost to me forever, I will use your feathers in my songs. You shall be of use to men on the earth. In days to come they shall use your beard and your feathers in all their ceremonies."

The turkey had flown from the eastern peak back to the land of The People. From it were descended all the turkeys that are tame in the world today. And all the useful and beautiful things the man saw in his pet turkey are still to be seen in all the turkeys that live today. In its feathers are the colors of the corn and the shining black of the rain cloud. The flash of the lightning and the gleam of the rainbow can be seen on its plumes when it walks in the sunlight. The darkness of the rain is in its beard, and the sign of the blue bean it carries on its forehead.

When the man came down from the mountain he found his corn very high. He pulled an ear of each of the four colors and took them to his wife in her hogan.

"But what is this?" she asked in surprise, for she had never seen corn before.

"This is the food of my people," the man said.

"But what do you do with it?" his wife asked.

"We have four ways with it when it is green. We put it in its husk in the hot coals of our fires so that it may roast. Or we take off the husk and roast the ear. We boil the ear in very hot water, or we cut off the kernels and make mush of them."

She cooked each ear in a different way and found that the corn had a very sweet taste. But when her father ate of it he was surprised and frightened. He could not imagine where his son-in-law found it. It was as delicious as fawn cheese. He told his daughter to find out how he could get some of the corn plants.

So Natínesthani took his wife to visit his farm. When they came to the top of a little hill, there it was stretched out before them in the sun. The rain began to fall gently on it, and above it came the span of a rainbow. They walked four times around the field in a circle as the sun went. The man showed her the white, blue and yellow corn and the corn of many colors. The yellow squashes he showed her too, and the melons and beans. The blue birds and the yellow birds were singing in the corn after the rain. And the farm was very beautiful, indeed. His wife said,

"I like your farm. Let us come here often for the corn and the beans and the melons and squash. You must teach me how to cook these too."

So he showed her what was to be eaten raw, and what was to be cooked, and how to do it. They walked among the tall corn plants, and he told her about the corn pollen. He told her it had many sacred uses. Then they gathered some more corn and went back to her hogan.

When she told her father about all the wonders she had seen he thanked her. He said he had lived long and traveled far, but he had never seen such things as these. He thanked her for such a rich son-in-law. Then he told her she must bring the man to visit their farm.

That night when they were alone together she gave him the message. She also asked him to reveal to her his sacred name, but he refused to do this. She asked him four times, and on the fourth time he asked her why she wanted to know his name. Then he told her his two names and asked her the name of her father and of herself. She said,

"He is called Piniltáni, the Deer Raiser, and I am known as Deer Raiser's Daughter."

In the morning she brought him new clothes which she had made for him. She had embroidered a yellow buckskin shirt with beads and fringed leggings of buckskin with strips of fur. She had worked moccasins with the quills of the porcupine and had made him a headdress adorned with great ears. When he had dressed himself they started out to the southeast to visit the farm of Deer Raiser. As they ascended a little hill she stooped and struck a large smooth stone with a turquoise wand she was carrying. Opening before them the man saw four steps leading to a hallway under the ground. They found themselves in a square rock house with four doorways of shining crystal, with a rainbow shining over each doorway. When she struck the eastern door with her wand they saw before them a vast and lovely land. It was as beautiful as the earth world, and more so. The man could not see the end of it. It was covered with flowers and filled with deer. The air was fragrant with the odor of blossoms and of pollen. Birds of many colors were flying around and nesting between the antlers of the deer. And great rainbows arched out all over the sky. The man said,

"It is very beautiful here, but it is not a farm. No man has planted anything here."

His wife took him through the three other doors. They all

led to other lands as beautiful as the first, and there were different animals in all of them. To the south there were antelopes. To the west there were mountain sheep, and to the north there were herds of elk.

In the center they found Deer Raiser waiting for them. He wanted to know how they liked his farm. When the man praised it very highly Deer Raiser killed a buck so that they could have meat to take home. He tied its legs with short rainbows after he had cut its throat with a stone arrow point. But Deer Raiser still wished to kill his son-in-law. He wanted his home to be as it was before the man came. He did not want his daughter to leave. He knew now that he could not kill him with tobacco or food, so he made ready another plan. In a canyon near by he had four fierce bears. He asked Natínesthani to go hunting there, telling him some deer had strayed into the canyon. The man agreed to go, but he stayed at the mouth of the canyon because the Wind People had warned him.

Deer Raiser urged him to go, but Natínesthani told him to go into the canyon himself, and he would stay at the mouth of it to catch the deer as they came out. After he had climbed a high rock he saw four large bears coming down the canyon and looking and smelling around. Deer Raiser had told them a man could be killed and eaten at the end of the canyon. The man just drew his lightning arrows and killed them. He called out to them as he did so,

"I am the God of the Bears. I am the Two Young Warrior Gods. I am too strong for you because The Gods are helping me."

Thus he gave himself great courage and his arrows went very straight indeed. Deer Raiser came running and panting. He was shouting out,

"Save a piece of the man for me."

He did not see his son-in-law until he was right there beside him.

Now Deer Raiser was a witch and a man-eater. He wanted some flesh of the man to eat, and he wanted some parts of the dead body to use in his witchcraft rites. But he knew now that his son-in-law was stronger than he was. However, he warned him not to hunt to the east and north. He did not want the man to gain the knowledge of all the peoples living in the country around there.

But He-Who-Teaches-Himself traveled far and wide in that country. He learned how to hunt in each direction, and he learned how to make the holy ceremonial cigarettes from the animals of each direction. He learned how to make many kinds of strong medicine to protect himself against all the evil ways of Deer Raiser.

The old witch-man Deer Raiser sought to make peace with him. He said,

"I will give up all my evil ways for you. I will seek your life no more. Treat me with all your powerful medicines. Let me hear all your songs and prayers. Teach me to smoke your tobacco."

So the man who had taught himself and who had learned to float on all the waters gave the first Feather Chant over his father-in-law, Deer Raiser. And he turned him into a good man.

Then he went back to visit his family. He taught all the songs and prayers to them and showed his younger brother how to become the medicine man of the new ceremony, known as the Feather Chant.

Then he went back to his farm and his wife near the lake where the logs had whirled round and round, in the little valley with the stream running through it. And some people say he still dwells there to this day.

EARTH MAN

THIS STORY is a very old one. It comes to us from the days when Nahóka Dinnéh, the Earth Man, was learning to hunt. It is from the Hotchónji, the chant which is used to drive away evil spirits.

Ma-i, the Coyote, was trailing Earth Man because he wanted his bow and arrows and the mask which he used when coming up to the deer. So Ma-i hid behind a bush when Earth Man was out hunting. When Earth Man drew near, Coyote threw his skin over him, and then he stole all the weapons.

Earth Man came to himself walking like an animal on all four feet. He was skulking about like a coyote, and he had the coyote smell on him. Since he was near the underground home of the White Squirrel People he crawled there to ask for help. The Squirrel People were angry and refused to listen to him. They did not want the coyote smell in their homes. Three times they threw him out, but the fourth time they knew it was an earth man in the form of a coyote, so they decided to help him. They made a large hoop of some grey willow wands and passed Earth Man through it. As he came out on the far side, the coyote skin began to crack over his head. They made a second hoop of coyote bush, and when the man passed through it the skin fell from his shoulders. After passing through a third hoop made of fresh fir, he was himself again down to his waist. And after he had gone through a fourth hoop, made of the cliff rose, he was a man again. But he had lost the power of speech.

Then Tóntso, the Harvest Fly, appeared. He was the messenger of The Gods. He said that only Black Wind could give a man his voice again, so he flew to the house of the Winds and brought Black Wind back with him. All the people gathered together and started to hold a ceremony over Earth Man. Black Wind sang as he worked, and covered his body with fresh pieces of fir and spruce. After a time Black Wind blew the pieces away, and Earth Man could speak again.

In the meantime Coyote was using the deer mask and the bows and arrows of the man. He was hunting all the time, but he only killed one rabbit. This was because he did not know how to use the weapons of Earth Man. He had gone to Earth Man's home, also, where he found the wife and two sons of the man. The wife and older son thought he was their husband and father, but the younger son was very doubtful. However, they all followed Coyote when he took them away to a new home.

When Earth Man was strong again, he took the trail to his own dwelling. He could not find any member of his family there, and he did not know what to do. He walked to the east searching for them. While he was resting under a bush he heard a voice speaking very clearly to him. It was the voice of his old fire-stick telling him not to be discouraged but to keep right on to the east. So he kept wandering and wandering and following the family trail. Once he heard the voice of an old family bowl speaking to him, and then that of a food basket. The fourth time he followed the advice of an old yucca brush which his wife had used. It told him to go toward the Blue Mountains.

Coyote had been moving the family around thinking to find better hunting places. He went to the east, then to the south, and then far down a river. Something was wrong with his hunting, and he could not find out what it was. He was very surprised when he came home one day to find the tracks of an earth man leading to his hogan.

Earth Man had found his way to the Blue Mountains, and he was very glad indeed to see his family again. But only his younger son knew him. He told his father all that Coyote had done. Earth

Man just settled down to wait for Coyote to come home from his hunting. He was very angry inside himself. But when Coyote came he said he was very glad to see the man again. He said he thought they could fix things up so that everyone would be happy. He asked the man to go with him to get some eagle feathers, so that they could make peace together. The man agreed, and they went together to find an eagle's nest on the top of a high, rocky point. As the man climbed and climbed Coyote made the rocks grow taller and taller. They became so high the Lightnings could play around them, and they seized the man and took him up to the cloud houses.

Coyote said, "Now I'll go home again."

But Tóntso had seen Earth Man on the rocks, and he flew swiftly to the rainbow house of The Gods. When he told them what had happened they said they would go to help their grandson, Earth Man. The Two Young Warrior Gods went searching for him through all the cloud houses and rock houses and wind houses. Finally they went through the mountain houses, but they could not find him anywhere.

Iknee, the Lightning, had taken Earth Man far away into the dark places. By the old road to the left, by the old red road of evil, through the four houses of darkness, he had taken the man to the home of Darkness Woman. By the road where a man's hair stands up high from its roots Iknee had taken him. An evil fire burned in her doorway and two evil spirits guarded the entrance to this house. When the man arrived at this unknown place he was afraid and trembled all over. He could not move his hands or his feet. So Talking God came swiftly and shook him four times and waved his prayer-sticks all around him. Then the man could come back to himself.

Talking God and the Two Young Warrior Gods brought Earth Man back again, and they sang their holy songs all the way. They walked back through the four houses and they taught him their songs so that he would know how to protect himself. Before they left him they told him that whenever he met Coyote he should always sing a certain song, and he should always begin to sing first. Then they went home on a rainbow.

Earth Man was very glad when he was with his family again. But he thought his hogan smelled of a strong evil smell. He wanted to get rid of Coyote once and forever. After thinking about it he baked rocks of four different colors and shapes in the fire. Then he ground them up with corn meal and cooked them again. After doing so he just settled down to wait until Coyote should come back from his hunting. He began to sing a song as Coyote stepped into the hogan.

"Come eat these cakes," he sang. "If you will eat these four cakes which I have baked for you, you may have my family and my weapons," he sang.

Now Ma-i, the Coyote, was very hungry after hunting and roaming all day. He just swallowed the four cakes right down, all of them. Then he ran about holding his stomach and shouting and suffering. He ran around the fire four times begging Earth Man to tell him what to do to get well. Coyote said he would take his skin on him again and his whiskers and his smell. He promised to go away forever and never to bother Earth Man and his family again. He would give back the bow and arrows and deer mask, and—but he died anyway, as he was running away. And far off down the canyon could be heard the howling of a coyote.

Earth Man built a new hogan, and he made a new bow and new arrows. He did not want to touch anything that Coyote had used. One day as he hunted he heard voices calling to him from the sky. Then one of the Wind Gods picked him up and took him to a cloud hogan high above the earth. A woman was sitting there waiting for him. She smiled and asked him why it had taken him so long to come to visit her. She gave him a suit of beautiful buckskin clothing which she had made for him. Then she began to prepare a pure white food for him to eat. He settled down beside her and told her how good it was to be in her home at last. The Spirit Wind warned him, however, to go slow about eating the food at first. So Earth Man just ate a few berries and waited. After a while he knew it was all right to eat the food. The Spirit Wind whispered to him that now the woman was ready to teach him all the songs she knew.

She was Spider Woman, and she taught Earth Man many songs and stories connected with a new ceremony which he was to give. She told him he was to be the first medicine man of the Hotchónji. She also taught him how to make fire in a new way before he went back to the earth. Then she made ready her web strings so that he could climb down to the horizontal land. He did not want to leave her, and he wondered if the web strings were strong enough to bear him. She blew on them four times, and they carried him safely down to the earth. When he arrived at his earth home he took four breath feathers and tied them to the web strings. Then he blew on them and sent them back to Spider Woman.

After this time he was taught many things by the Spirit Wind. He learned how to make the hoops for the new rite and how to choose the wood of which they were to be made. He learned how to tie the breath feathers to the wood, and how to make the prayer-sticks.

One day he met Natsitclóseh, the big bird which is called Road Runner. This bird said he was going to a moccasin game which was to begin in four days. It was to be between the animals of the day and the animals of the night in a big corral made of a circle of fresh green boughs. When Earth Man arrived at the place he saw all the night animals sitting in the northern part of the corral and all the day animals in the southern part. Owl was chief of the night animals and Fox was chief of the day animals. They sat facing each other in two rows. Between them was a row of moccasins buried in the earth so that only their tops showed.

Now the animals of the night wanted it to be dark always. They could see better and hunt better at night. They were happier in the nighttime. They wished to have the day become night, too. But the day animals wanted to have it always light. They said that they could be happy only in the light of the sun and the day.

If the Night People won the game they said that the Sun Bearer had better come down out of the sky. If the Day People won they said he was to stay up there all the time.

They painted a flat piece of yucca wood black on one side and white on the other. Then they had a tossup to see which side would start the game. The white side turned up, so the Day People started by hiding a small stone in one of the moccasins. They hung an old blanket up while they were hiding the stone. The Night People guessed and guessed where the stone was. The Night Hawk finally found its place, so his side won the stone and hid it. All the time they were singing songs. Each animal had a song of its own. There was not a creature in the world which did not have a song of its own. There was not a creature which crept or flew or walked or crawled in the sky world or the earth world which did not have a song of its own. And each animal tried to sing well, for it might bring luck to its side. First Owl sang to tell his love for the night and the great darkness.

> O, I wish not the end
> Of all the nights!
> O, I wish not the end
> Of all the nights!
> May the last night
> Of all time endure forever!

The Night People kept the stone so long Gopher decided to steal it. He burrowed down under the ground and made a little path along the row of moccasins. Whenever a night animal guessed right he quickly moved the stone to another moccasin. So the Day People kept it a long time. Then Antelope sang a song.

> Lo, I am the light brown one!
> Truly in the distant glade,
> Below, through the opening
> In the far green trees
> The Antelope wanders.

Then Ground Squirrel sang.

> Slender and striped,
> Slender and striped,
> Look at him standing up there!
> He stands up there
> So slender in his stripes—
> The Squirrel in his little white shirt!

When Gopher became tired Bat won the stone. The game went on and on. First one side had it and then the other. Toward morning the song of Magpie was heard.

> Listen now to the Magpie!
> Listen now to the Magpie!
> Here, below, within,
> In the white of his wings
> Lie the footsteps of the morning!
> In his trail is the morning light.
> It dawns! It dawns!

And when the curtain of day was rising, the game was a tie between the animals of the day and of the night. And each one fled away to his home in the forest, in the desert, in the rocks. And they said that they would never meet again. So we still have the light and the darkness, just as it was in the beginning.

While the animals were running away to their homes Earth Man heard a very strange rumbling noise. Red Bird heard it first as he was flying to his home over the mesa. Then everyone listened, for they heard it growing louder and louder. They looked to the north and saw two round white things rolling toward them from a great distance. Everyone wondered what this meant, for they saw that the objects were two white skulls. When the Sun Bearer came he told them that they were the skulls of twin brothers who had been killed long ago by the men of Taos. Everyone stood silent, not knowing what to do. But Tóntso went to get Talking God.

After hearing about what had happened, Talking God and some of the other gods went first to Taos. They had to find out all that they could about the two bodies which belonged to the skulls. They found them in many pieces strewn about some rocks, and there was no flesh on the bones nor blood in the veins. The Gods told Tóntso to go to call the Black Ant People together. These ran all over the rocks and collected the missing flesh and blood, placing it on some buckskins The Gods had put together. Then the Messenger Fly went everywhere, far and wide to all the holy places, to all those who could bring life back again. He called the spirits of the earth, of the clouds and of the lightning. He called the spirits of the corn and of the life pollen, of the rainbow, and of the sun and of the dawn. He called the inner beings of everything out of which the body and spirit of man are made.

They all gathered at the place where the game had been played. In the brush corral Talking God, the grandfather of The Gods, arranged everything very carefully. He spent twelve days doing all this, and Spider Woman came to help him. They had all the parts of the two men who had been killed on two new white buckskins. They saw that the Black Ants put the veins and the arteries back in the right places, and after this they blew the blood back. The Gods stepped back and forth over the buckskins. The Spirit Wind blew into the nostrils. The bodies of the men began to move and to breathe. Slowly they became stronger and stronger. But they were still very weak. Then The Gods made the four wooden hoops and put the men through these. They could stand up now, but they were not yet able to walk. Then Tóntso said to them, "I think I know what is the matter with you. Your shadows must be very sick indeed. It is your shadows which are making you so weak."

After this The Gods took a very beautiful white feather and put many fine offerings on it. They put sacrifices of turquoise beads, and white shell, and jet and abalone shell on the feather, and they placed it below a tree which had been struck by lightning—pointing it carefully to the east. Then they all prayed to cure this weakness caused by the sick shadows of the two men. And the men became whole again.

This was the custom of curing long ago. They made sure that the shadows were cured, too.

The Two Young Warrior Gods made arrows out of young shoots of fir and pine, and they treated the two men with these. Then they sent them up into the mountains to live. Talking God and the other gods taught the songs and ceremonies to Earth Man, and after this he was ready to give the Hotchónji, the chant for driving away evil spirits.

THE DREAMER

THIS STORY is about Bitáhatani, the Dreamer, who, even as a little boy, had many dreams and saw many visions. It begins near the canyon of Tségihi. High up in its cliffs were the homes of the ancient people. One day Bitáhatani saw tall beings dancing in big blue masks on the tops of the cliffs. He heard the songs of the Holy Ones standing in the high places. But when he told his family of these strange things they would not believe him. They said he was making things up and would not listen to him. His mother wondered within herself, however, as she knew that only the far, mysterious ones, known as the Yei, or Holy People, wore the big blue masks.

His mother's family belonged to the clan of the Thatsíni, and they were a family of hunters. They lived in a hogan near Tségihi, in a place called Where-The-Waters-Are-Red. He was the third of four brothers, and he had an older sister and a brother-in-law. No one of them guessed that Bitáhatani was to become a great chanter. Sometimes his younger brother, Nakíestsai, seemed to listen to his stories, but the others made so much fun of him it became his custom to go off on lonely paths by himself. On one of these trails, as he was sleeping under a juniper bush, he dreamed he was dancing with Mountain Sheep People and hearing the songs of the spirit world.

When he was about fifteen or sixteen his older brothers started off on a big hunt. They told him to stay home and dream, but he followed them a few hours later. As night came on, their trail became very dim, so he built himself a little brush shelter in a canyon and started a fire with his fire-stick. He had seen the tracks of turkey and many deer and hoped to tell his brothers of these signs. Just as he was about to fall asleep he heard people singing and talking. He thought a ceremony must be beginning. Some of the Crow People seemed to be flying in and out of a cave in the canyon bank above him. They were calling back and forth to other people in a cave on the opposite bank.

"They say, they say, they say, they say," he heard repeated four times.

"What do they say?" he heard in answer four times. Then the singing and calling stopped and there was quiet in the canyon.

About midnight the Dreamer waked up. He saw sparks of fire being thrown across the canyon above him. He heard a voice saying,

"They wandered too close to the homes of the Earth People. Twelve of the Deer People have been killed."

"Is that what happened?"

"I hear that one of the Crow and one of the Magpie People have been killed, too."

These questions and answers were called back and forth, and then the Dreamer saw tall figures passing from the caves on what seemed to be a swinging bridge of red and blue cords. Someone would ask a question four times and then the answer would come four times.

"Did they kill the crow who ate along the backbone of the deer?"

"Yes, the marrow-eater is dead, too."

"Did they shoot the bird who sits between the horns?"

"Yes, they killed the magpie who was the friend of the deer and played between his horns."

"Twelve deer, did they say?"

"Yes, but that will be all the hunting they will get for a long time."

"Yes, the four men have killed all that they may kill."

"It is well. Let us begin the songs and dancing."

Crow men and women were standing facing each other, just

as the dancers of the Night Chant stand opposite to each other today. For this was the beginning of the Night Chant—or Yeibechai, as some people call it—and the lines of the fires today stand for the opposite banks of the canyon which the Dreamer saw first. He was to be the first medicine man of the new ceremony, but he did not know this as yet. He watched through the rest of the night as the singing and dancing continued. As the dawn came he heard the bluebird song, and with this the dancing ended. Before the sun rose he saw great flocks of crows flying forth from the caves in all directions. Then he started out to find his three brothers and his brother-in-law because he knew they were the hunters about whom the Crow People had been talking.

He arrived at their camp early in the morning and found only his youngest brother there, guarding the bodies of twelve slain deer. When the others came in from hunting they had nothing with them. They all sat around the fire eating roast meat; then they smoked and talked and joked with the Dreamer.

"Where were you yesterday, Brother Prophet? We thought we left you home asleep and dreaming," they said.

"I followed your trail and heard about your hunting last night," answered the Dreamer.

"How could you do that? Where were you? This is just another of your foolish stories," they said.

Bitáhatani told them of the strange things he had seen and heard, but they would not believe him. He told them that they would kill no more deer, but they just laughed at him. However, as he started on his way home, he thought that his youngest brother had listened a little. He told his mother and father of the dancing and singing he had heard and of what the Crow People had said about the Earth People who were hunting. His parents sat very quietly and thoughtfully. When the other brothers returned, the mother told them to pay attention to the story of the Dreamer. They had killed nothing after the twelve deer and the crow and the magpie which had alighted on the carcasses.

The brother-in-law had been thinking about the words of Bitáhatani, too. He was beginning to believe that the Dreamer was a man of true visions. His older brothers knew that he spoke truly because he had described the deer and the crow and the magpie, but they did not want to believe him when he said that they would kill no more deer at this time. The oldest brother said that Bitá-hatani had not made the deer, and that he could not move them from place to place. He said they would go on another hunting trip and get much deer and game. But the brother-in-law said he would not go, that he would not tire himself out with useless work. The youngest brother said he would stay at home too.

When the curtains of day began to part, the two older brothers started out. The brother-in-law and Nakíestsai stayed home with the Dreamer. When the yellow evening light came the hunters returned empty-handed. For four mornings they went out thinking they would surely get some deer. For four evenings they returned with not even a ground squirrel. They were very angry and blamed the Dreamer for their bad luck. They sat by the fire and smoked, and would not speak to him.

A few days later they all went out together, and, as they were resting on the top of a cliff, they saw four Rocky Mountain sheep picking their way among the rocks below them. When the sheep disappeared the oldest brother told the Dreamer to go down into the canyon to track them. He ran down and hid behind a mountain mahogany bush, drawing his bow as he did so. He placed his arrow in position, but he could not draw it as he saw the sheep coming up the trail. He began to tremble, and his arm grew numb. After a while he tracked the sheep again and hid behind a bush of coyote corn. Again the sheep approached and again he could not let the arrow fly. A sharp pain ran through his arms and legs. The third time he went to head off the sheep he hid behind a juniper bush. But again they passed by unharmed, and again, a fourth time, as he hid behind a cherry tree.

His brothers were watching from above. They wondered why he did not shoot the big-horned sheep who seemed to pass so near to him. They saw him behaving in a strange way, rubbing his arms and legs and running along the trail. But after the fourth appearance of the sheep they saw him no more. Just as the Dreamer was ready to draw his bow the fourth time he looked up at the sheep, and saw that they were the Holy Ones known as the Ganáskidi, the Mountain Sheep Gods. There they stood in their great blue masks with their black buckskin bags on their backs—four of them, two gods and two goddesses. And they smiled and greeted him. They told him to strip himself of his old clothes, and they dressed him in new buckskin garments like their own and placed a large blue mask on his head. So he left his earthly garments just as they fell, his left moccasin to the left with his left legging, his bow and his quiver of arrows, his right moccasin to the right with the right legging, his shirt and his head-band, and the arrow he had been about to shoot.

The Gods fed him with sacred corn meal and made him holy by throwing their breath all around him. Then they took four steps with him to the edge of the cliff. When they had all stepped off the cliff they traveled on a rainbow to the place where the Holy Ones live. Here Hastyéyalti, the Talking God and maternal grandfather of the gods, was waiting for them with Hastyéhogan, the Home God. They had sent Tóntso, the Messenger Fly, to tell the other gods that a man of the Earth People had come to be made holy and to learn the new ceremony. So twelve of the chief gods and goddesses had soon gathered together, and also many birds and animals. Of course Coyote was there and passing in and out of the medicine hogan. Everyone left his bows and arrows and extra bundles outside the hogan, but a little wind told the Dreamer to watch his belongings whenever Coyote was around. Inside the holy hogan he saw that The Gods were preparing baskets of sacred objects and making prayer-sticks. He began to notice everything very carefully. He promised twelve large buckskins to them if they would teach him the prayers and songs. They agreed to do this, and everything was made ready.

Now his brothers had found the place where he had left his old clothing. But they could find no trace of their brother from this spot, and they were afraid that they had lost him. They went home to prepare sacrifices which they took to the place of his disappearance. They took baskets of turquoise, white shell, cannel coal and abalone shell. They took baskets of iron ore, blue pollen, life pollen and corn pollen to the place where the garments lay, and they prayed and sang to Talking God that they might have news of their brother. After this the Spirit Wind told them the Dreamer would return to them on the fourth day after that one, so they all returned home. On the fourth night, while they were watching and praying, they sang some new songs which they had learned from the Wind. They cast the sacred corn meal in the four directions. Just as they were finishing the bluebird song which says, "I am walking in the morning," the Dreamer's step was heard, and there he was in the eastern doorway. So that is the reason why, when The People give the Night Chant today, they stay awake on the fourth night, and they call it "His Sleepless Night." The fifth day is called "The Dreamer's Day," and after this the preparations are made for the sand paintings and for the visitors who will come to the ceremony.

When the Dreamer was back on the horizontal earth plane The Gods sent messengers to bring in the offerings which had been made to them on the edge of the canyon. They filled five large bowls with the offerings. The fifth bowl was filled with rock crystal, for the gods had the power of taking any small piece of stone or shell and making it grow to any size or quantity they wished. They covered the bowls with the new buckskins and sang over them, dancing around each of them in the four directions. The Dreamer listened and watched very carefully. It is said that he learned the songs in less time than any man who has ever tried to do so.

Early on the morning of the sixth day they began the sand painting of the whirling logs with the holy lake in the center. The Gods drew this first on a piece of woven cotton cloth. They told the Dreamer to fix the lines and colors very carefully in his inner mind. They told him he could make the painting later in colored sands on the floor of the medicine hogan, but they could not let him have the real painting. They said it was full of their power, and that they could not trust it to the careless Earth People. They said that if it were torn or hurt in any way the corn might not grow up or the rain fall down. On the seventh day they showed him the picture of the dancing gods with the Talking God and the Water Bearer, and on the eighth day the picture with the four Mountain Sheep Gods. During the nights which passed between the making and the destroying of these pictures they turned the baskets down and drummed on them with yucca drumsticks, singing the songs which belong to the pictures and preparing the sacred medicine mixed with the holy water. The Dreamer learned later that these songs were to cure headaches, sore eyes and paralysis of the legs.

On the ninth night, just as they were getting ready for the dance to which all The People come, one of the Holy Ones called the Dreamer aside and spoke to him softly for some time. After this they went off together into the sky world in four left-handed spiral paths. They were visiting the mountains of the four directions when Talking God missed the Dreamer. He thought that Coyote must have taken him away for no good reason, and he went searching for him. He went to the summits of all the mountains until he came to the northern one. There Tóntso, the Messenger Fly, who was staying with the Bear People on the top of the mountain, told him that he was on the right trail if he wanted to find his grandchild. So Talking God threw some sunbeam ladders up against the sky and climbed up them into the sky houses of The Gods. He met some eagles and other birds who said they had not seen the Dreamer, but just then he heard someone singing a song, and it was one of the songs which the Dreamer had been learning. Talking God searched around and found his grandchild under a shelf in one of the sky houses. Seizing him by the leg and arm he began to descend the sky ladders with him and brought him back to the earth in four right-handed spiral paths.

The Gods rejoiced when they saw that the Dreamer had returned to them, and they began the dance of the ninth night which they had not been able to hold before this time. The Dreamer looked around him and saw that he was surrounded by all kinds of Holy People. He sang a song saying,

> I am walking on the tops of the mountains.
> The Gods are before me.
> The Gods are behind me.
> I am walking in the midst of The Gods.

There was much feasting and dancing on the ninth night, but toward the end of it he began to feel sad and to long to see his family. So The Gods told him he could go home to his mother's hogan in the morning if he could repeat all the songs he had heard. When he had done so they told him to go home to teach all of his knowledge to the Earth People. Just as the birds began to sing in the morning he started on his way. He had not gone far when he heard an owl calling. The owl told him there was one thing he had not learned and that was how to make the fragrant incense to spread on the hot coals during the curing ceremonies in the medicine hogan. The owl showed him how this was done and then directed him to go to the place on the edge of the canyon where he had left his clothing, and to pray there.

His family was very glad to see him, and he stayed with them for some time. He was very glad to see them too, but every night as he sang the songs of The Gods to them they seemed to go to sleep and to be unable to learn them. He sang them for three nights, and no one learned a single song. On the fourth night he said, "It is because you do not pay me that you can remember nothing." So the eldest brother gave the Dreamer twelve large buckskins from unwounded deer which had been smothered in sacred pollen. All the time the singing had been going on Nakíestsai, the youngest brother, seemed to be asleep behind the grandmother. But he had been singing the songs all the time within himself and he now sang them through without making a mistake.

In the meantime many people had heard that the Dreamer knew a new ceremony which would cure many ills and put one back on the pollen path of The Gods. They began to gather outside his hogan and beg him to help them. A man came who said that his son had lost his sight, and another who said that his son had headaches and was deafened. Another man came who said that his daughter's legs were stiff and unable to move, and another who said that his child had a crooked mouth. They offered the Dreamer many gifts if he would perform the new ceremony. He ordered a new hogan to be built and showed his youngest brother how to help him. And in the end the patients of the rites recovered and walked again in beauty.

After these first performances of the Night Chant for the Earth People the Dreamer told his youngest brother that he was to be the medicine man of the chant and ordered him to prepare for a great ceremony. So his family gathered wood and water and prepared a great deal of food for the people who would come. Many of the Holy Ones arrived for this ceremony and watched Nakíestsai conduct it in a worthy manner. When it was over and The Gods had departed, The People looked around for the Dreamer, but he had disappeared. The Gods had taken him home with them, and he was never seen on earth again. But before he left he said goodbye to his youngest brother and told him not to weep for him. He told him he was going to live forever after in the home of The Gods in a place where he could watch over his people. He told him he would hear his voice in the voice of the thunders and know that he was near when the rain blessed the land and the corn grew tall.

IN THE GARDEN OF
THE HOME GOD

ONCE UPON A TIME, in the ancient days, there was a Home God named Hastyéhogan who lived at Broad Rock in the Canyon de Chelly in Arizona. This canyon had very high cliffs on either side of it, and there were houses built right into the rocky sides of it by people of the olden days.

One spring day Hastyéhogan went out with his family to prepare his garden and his farm. He had a wife named Wise-Woman-Who-Weaves, a little boy named Dawn Boy and a little girl named Rainbow Girl. They came to a place where the earth had washed out from a crevice in the cliffs.

"Here is a smooth slope all ready for the planting," the Home God said. And he cut a long stick from a cherry tree and made it into a planting-stick. As he did this he was singing a song. He sang a song to the ancient people who had lived in the canyon, to the warm, brown earth of the canyon, and then he even sang a song to his planting-stick. Now in those days songs were very important. You sang a song to explain everything you were doing. People didn't talk so much. They even prayed with songs. They sang songs to Father Sky and Mother Earth, to the rain clouds and the corn spirits, to the Turquoise Goddess and to all the animals. They sang songs to each other. When you sang a song you put all the power of your heart in it, and it was a holy thing.

While Home God was singing, Dawn Boy and Rainbow Girl made themselves planting-sticks and began to help him. They broke the ground carefully and began to plant the corn seeds. And they began to sing, too. The corn seeds were of many different colors. There were blue corn seeds and pink, dark grey and red, and yellow and purple, and corn seeds of all colors.

Here is a song the Home God sang:

> I am planting the blue corn seed.
> So, I am planting it.
> It will grow quickly in one night.
> It will grow and flourish.
> In great beauty it will increase
> In the garden of the Home God.

So they all sang the song, and the corn began to grow before their very eyes. By the time they left the field it was almost as tall as the little boy.

The next day Hastyéhogan sent a friend of his, the Harvest God, to look at it. The name of the Harvest God was Ganáskidi. He had a big, black buckskin bag on his back to hold all the good things of the fields. He wore mountain-sheep horns and red woodpecker feathers on his head. Ganáskidi came back and told Home God that the corn was all ready to pick. So they called Hastyéyalti, who was the chief of the gods in the canyon, to come with them to see the corn. He was also called the Talking God because he explained things to the other gods. He was the grandfather of the mother of the gods, so you can see how old he was. He wore twelve eagle feathers on his head, and he carried a tobacco pouch made of squirrel skin.

The little boy and the little girl were very surprised to see the corn grown so tall. The corn tassels were all in bloom, and the ears of corn were ripe. There were beautiful birds of all kinds flying around in the corn patch. So they all sang a song about coming to visit the corn. Dawn Boy asked his father why the corn had ripened so rapidly. And his father told him that the water of the dark rain clouds had made it grow. Rainbow Girl then asked her mother why the corn had ripened so rapidly. And her mother told

her the water of the dark mist had made it grow. Then a beautiful
rainbow spread over the garden of the Home God. So they sang
another song to thank the rain and the mist and the rainbow and
the sun.

The song began like this:

> With the water of the dark cloud
> See the blue corn grow!
> With the water of the dark mist
> See the white corn grow!
> With this it grows.
> With this it is beautiful!

Dawn Boy said, "Father, the land looks beautiful with the
corn. Why does it look so beautiful?" The Home God said, "I'll
tell you in a song." And he sang another song about the corn. The
little boy listened very happily. He liked his father's songs. So
he asked him again why the corn grew so fast. Thus it is with
children. They ask many questions. And when they are answered
they ask them all over again.

This little Dawn Boy loved to ask questions of his father,
Home God, and he loved to hear his father answer them in singing
words. This time the father sang about the yellow pollen on the
corn tassels. Rainbow Girl also asked her mother the same questions, and Wise Woman told her the corn ate the dew from the
dark mist. Then Rainbow Girl asked some more questions. For
that is the way with little girls. They ask just as many questions
as little boys. In fact, some people think they ask more.

Now they were all wandering through the field and singing.
They came to a place where a new plant was growing. Home God
said it was a bean plant. It was covered with little blossoms, and
small pods had begun to form on it. Dawn Boy looked at his
father and said, "What is this, my father, which waves so beautifully in the breeze?" Hastyéhogan said to him, "That is the
reaching tendril of the blue bean plant."

And he sang him a song which went like this:

> The great bean plant
> Grows with the corn.
> Its rootlets now
> Grow with the corn.
> Its blossoms now
> Are with the corn.
> Its pollen now
> Is with the corn.
> And now its seed
> Is with the corn.
> The great bean plant
> Grows with the corn.

They kept on walking in the garden and fields, and soon they came to a place where large, round, yellow flowers were growing. The children asked what these were, and the father told them they were the blossoms of the squash plant. Then he sang them a song about the squash plant growing with the corn and the bean plants. Even as Dawn Boy and Rainbow Girl watched, the blossoms began to change from yellow to white. And then they began to wither. Soon beautiful, round squashes began to form. And the children wanted to know if they could pick some of them. They sang a song like this:

> Shall we pick the fruit
> Of the great squash vine?
> Shall I pick it?
> Shall you pick it?
> Shall we break off the fruit
> Of the great squash vine?
> Shall we pick it up?
> Shall I?
> Shall you?

After they picked the squash they ran to pick some beans. And they also discovered some sweetly smelling tobacco blossoms. While the children were doing this Wise Woman and The Gods in the garden began to pick the corn. And they tied it all together with some strings of white lightning and strings of the rainbow. Just then a shower was seen approaching, and the children ran to their parents. Home God sang a song as they started to go to their hogan. And this is what he sang:

> Truly in the east
> The great bean
> And the blue corn
> Are tied with the white lightning.
> Listen!
> The rain comes!
> The voice of the bluebird is heard!

> Truly in the west
> The blue bean
> And the great squash
> Are tied with the rainbow.
> Listen!
> The rain comes!
> The voice of the bluebird is heard!

You see the bluebird means happiness to people because it sings as the dawn comes, and so they were very glad indeed to hear his voice. The water now lay in pools under the corn. And everyone rejoiced. The Home God sang a very special song:

> From the top of the great corn
> The water splashes,
> Down, down.
> I hear it.
> Around the roots of the great corn
> The water foams,
> Around, around.
> I see it.

Wise Woman said to her husband, Home God, "You have a very beautiful farm. I like your corn and squash and beans. I thank you for them." So then he sang another song, just for her. They were a very happy family. When they were sitting down around the fire in the center of their hogan they all began to tell about the day's adventures. Dawn Boy and Rainbow Girl were happy because their father had such a farm. They kept asking their patient father more and more questions. They wanted to know what was happening now in his wonderful garden. After they had had a good meal of corn bread and stewed peaches they begged to see the rain falling on the farm again. So the father took them to a little hill near the hogan where they could watch the raindrops splashing on the corn. And they could see the Rainbow Goddess again circling the little field and protecting it. The father sang:

> The corn grows up.
> The rain falls down.
> The waters of the dark clouds
> Drop, drop!
> The corn grows up.
> The rain falls down.
> The water of the dark mist
> Drips, drips!
> Someone is beating
> Against the sky.
> I hear it!
> I hear it!
> Fall, rain, fall!
> Grow, corn, grow!

Then the children heard the voice of the thunder and saw the great sky serpents of the lightning. Dawn Boy asked his father who was making that noise. The father sang:

> Thonah! Thonah!
> There is a voice above,
> The voice of the thunder.
> Within the dark cloud
> Again and again it sounds.
> Thonah! Thonah!

Aiena! Aiena!
There is a voice below,
The voice of the grasshopper.
Among the plants
Again and again it sounds.
Aiena! Aiena!

Dawn Boy said, "I like those sounds when you sing about them. Sing some more songs, please." While they sat on the top of the little hill and watched the rainbow, Home God sang to them. They were getting very sleepy now. The Home God put his right arm around Dawn Boy and his left arm around Rainbow Girl. He sheltered them under his blanket while he sang to them.

Oh, beautiful upon the earth,
All things are growing.
I hear the voice
That quickens now the earth.
So, happily may we return
To our waiting home!
All things are growing!

Then the shower was over, and the rainbow disappeared. And a fresh, gentle wind was blowing. The Moon Goddess came out and shone gently on them over the distant, dark mountains and dim, white cliffs of the canyon.

"It is time to go to sleep now," called Wise Woman. So the children went to their hogan to lie on the soft blankets their mother had woven for them. As the Home God sat by the fire across from his wife, he sang to them the last song:

Lulla-lay, lulla-lay,
Go to sleep, go to sleep!
May all your dreams be happy!
In the place of the night
Soon the dawn-light will come.

The curtains of daylight
Will hang over our home.
Now sleep, little Dawn Boy,
And little Rainbow Girl.
Lulla-lay, lulla-lay!

And the moon shone gently down over the happy, sleeping family and the garden of the Home God.

THE SNAKE WOMAN

IN THE DAYS beyond memory they say there was a Snake Chant of The People. Today only parts of it can be remembered by very old men and women. The songs and prayers were in a language which no one can understand today. It is spoken of as the "changed meaning" language, and it must be learned syllable by syllable by the medicine men of the present day. They say part of it remains in Enemy Way Chant, and in the Hozóni, the Chant of Beauty—in the female part of this chant, which is called the Chant of Earthly Beauty. The other part, the male half of the chant, is called the Chant of Heavenly Beauty. It is hard to give the meaning even of the names of these parts of this chant in another language. These two parts really form a whole called Beauty Way Chant. But this word for beauty means many things. It means beauty within as well as beauty without. It means peacefulness within and without. It means doing things in the right way of harmony between The Gods and The People. If you are "hozóni" you are walking on the pollen path, the path of blessing from the gods.

If you want to see the sand paintings of the Chant of Beauty you have to be in the land of The People for four autumns. They say that there are sixteen of them and that they have many snakes appearing in them. Instead of a hero going on a journey to gain new knowledge for his people, it is a girl named Glíshpah who goes to the underground land of the Snake People and learns how to conduct a new ceremony. She became the first medicine woman of the Chant of Beauty. She is called Snake Woman.

The story begins, however, with four men who wished to travel to the western ocean. They wanted to go back there to see what the great western water was like and to learn its ways of power. They were desert people, but they had heard of the great water from their grandfathers.

They were Bear Man, Snake Man, Frog Man and Turtle Man, and they kept traveling on over mountains and sand hills, keeping always toward the yellow horizontal west. They wanted to touch the power of the great water, to stand in it and thereafter have water power. But as they went they began to have a very difficult time because they met many Enemy People. Frog Man and Turtle Man decided to turn back and go home, but Bear Man and Snake Man kept right on going. One day they heard about two beautiful girls who were looking for husbands. They were the daughters of two chiefs who were holding an arrow-shooting contest. The two men who could shoot farthest were to be the husbands—so the fathers said.

Now Bear Man and Snake Man seemed to be two very old men. They stumbled as they walked along, and they coughed and sneezed all the time. They went to the place where the shooting was going on, and, although water was streaming from their eyes and their arms trembled, nevertheless their arrows went way beyond the arrows of the younger men. The fathers of the two girls were very sad when they saw this happening. They did not want to give their beautiful daughters to such old men. They decided to give a feast and dance and to let the girls choose their own husbands from the men assembled there.

So Glíshpah and Bispáli, the other girl, began sway-singing and encircling the men—the way they do today in the War Dance. They became very hot and tired and slipped out of the dance in order to go to a little stream to get a drink. As they did so they heard a strange sound and smelled a very fragrant odor. It was like nothing they had ever smelled before. They wandered around trying to find it, and as they did so they saw a light shining toward the north. When they came to the brush shelter where the light was they saw two handsome young men lying there. They had their backs to the fire from which the light came, and they were smoking their pipes. The one in the northern part of the shelter was Bear Man, and the one in the southern part, Snake Man. But they were young again.

Bear Man was dressed in black and brown fur and Snake Man wore a soft garment of many different colors. They both had great necklaces of turquoise and white shell beads, and they smoked pipes made of turquoise and white stone. The girls stood there admiring them very much, but the men paid no attention to them. They just went right on smoking, and it was from their pipes that the sweet-smelling smoke was coming. The two girls went to sit beside them. Bispáli sat down beside Bear Man in the northern part of the shelter and Glíshpah beside Snake Man in the southern part. They asked the men for a smoke of the sweet tobacco, but the men paid no attention until they had asked for the tobacco four times. Then Bear Man passed his stone pipe to Bispáli and Snake Man his turquoise pipe to Glíshpah. The two girls liked the sweet tobacco so much they forgot everything else. They just crawled under the blankets of the two men and spent the night there.

But everything was different in the morning. When the two girls woke up they were frightened, for the men were old again. Snake Man and Bear Man were snoring beside them with their mouths open. A few old yellow fangs were all that they had for teeth. Bispáli and Glíshpah rose quietly and tried to run away. Glíshpah was tied, however, by a big, blue racer snake to the old Snake Man, and Bispáli found a brown furry arm holding her fast to Bear Man. They broke away after much trouble and tried to run in the direction of their homes. They could hear the voices of their people calling them, and they tried to call back in answer. But wherever they ran the smoke from the tobacco of Bear Man and Snake Man followed them.

The journey of Bispáli, who married Bear Man, goes on from here in a different story. It is part of another ceremony called the Mountain Chant. The two girls decided to separate, and

Bear Woman went to the east while Snake Woman started westward.

"Goodbye, my sister," they called to each other.

"Whatever you must do, do it well," they said.

"Sometime our paths may cross again."

Later when the two men came to the place where their wives had separated they knew the very spot. The tobacco trails went in opposite directions.

Snake Woman had to walk through mud and water as she went west. At last she came to the Place of Emergence. Here there was a lake with an island in the middle of it, and she thought she would like to reach this island. While she stood on the shore of the lake two Snake People came up out of the water to talk to her. They told her they lived in an underwater land of great beauty and invited her to visit it with them. Glíshpah did not know it, but this was the home of Klíshtso, the Great Snake, or Snake Man, as she had known him. When she went under the water she found a wide and pleasant land with many cornfields all over it. There were blue mountains in the distance and many birds of different colors were flying around. The Snake People took her to a large hogan which had four rooms. They invited her to sit down on a pile of new white buckskins and they fed her corn pollen from a little bowl which never grew empty. No matter how hungry she was, there the little bowl was, full of good corn pollen. She stayed in each of the four rooms in turn, and she enjoyed herself very much.

One night there was a great feast. While she was sitting on her pile of buckskins a handsome young man entered the hogan and came to sit down beside her. It was Snake Man, and he was young again, as he was the first time she had seen him. She was very glad inside herself while they ate together and laughed together. He asked her why she had run away from him. She should know that he was both young and old, just as he wanted to be. He thought that they should always be together from that day on. He said he wanted to teach her the Hozóni, or Chant of Beauty. If she would stay with him he would teach her the story and the songs and other parts of the ceremony. It was October then, and he taught her to make four big sand paintings which belonged to the first part of the rite. As he worked he sang the songs for her and showed her how to use the sands on the painting. All through the winter she learned the various parts of the rite. But when spring came she began to get lonely and wanted to see her own people. She asked Snake Man if she should go to visit her family. He said that she must go back to them in order to teach the new ceremony to her younger brother, Grey Boy. As she started across the mountains she heard someone calling her. It was Old Man Owl who asked her where she was going and what she was doing. So she told him who she was and said she was just traveling. But he knew all about her and her home, anyway. He told her never to be in a hurry but to learn from all the Animal People whom she met. He himself would teach her how to make the incense for the new rite and how to make all the medicine needed in the Hozóni. She must learn first how to make his sacrifice and his prayer-stick, and to know what his particular song meant.

When she arrived at her mother's house her family was very glad to see her. Her mother cried because she had thought Glíshpah dead long ago. Her mother laughed and cried over her, and it made Glíshpah glad to see her again. She told the family all that had happened to her and all that she had learned. She said she would show them how to have the Hozóni, that she would teach Grey Boy all that he needed to know to become a medicine man.

So they sprinkled corn meal over her as she sang. She taught her brother very carefully, but he seemed not to be able to learn the songs and prayers. One morning she shelled some corn and put a kernel down in front of him for each song. Then she ground the corn and made a mush of it for her brother. So he ate all the songs and prayers, and after that he found that he knew every sound in them. One by one she showed him sixteen sand paintings, four of which were to be given each autumn for four years. Then she showed him how to make and paint the kethawns, or prayer-sticks, with which to invite The Gods to come to the Hozóni. After this she sang the whole ceremony over him again to make him into a medicine man. For four nights she showed him how to tie and untie the knots. For four mornings they had the ceremonial baths. There were four days of sand painting, and they sang all through the last night. As the Hozóni ended they took the dawn into themselves, facing the east and the new light. Then all the people who had gathered went away to their homes.

Glíshpah said farewell to her mother and brother and family. She longed to see her husband again, so she started back over the mountains. She walked through the water and the mud and came at last to the home of the Great Snake, her husband. And he was very glad to see her, and there under the lake she dwells with him forever.

THE LAST OF THE MONSTERS

THE YOUNG WARRIOR GODS were tired of killing monsters. They thought that they would rest for four days at the home of their mother, the Turquoise Woman. Moreover, they had not seen their father, the Sun Bearer, for eight days. They needed to learn further ways of greater power which only he could show them. The Spirit Wind had whispered to Nayenezgáni, the elder brother, of another enemy monster, The - Bear - Who - Tracks-People, and of the strange being called the Traveling Stone. They had heard of colored creatures who lived under rocks, and brown giants of the earth, and of old, ruined cities so filled with animals and large black birds that people could live in them no longer.

Elder Brother asked his mother where the great bear lived, but she refused to tell him. Instead, she tried to picture to him the power of the enemy he sought. She was frightened. She did not want her sons to risk their lives again. She wanted them to stay at home in her hogan and live on the pollen path of peace. Three times Elder Brother asked her concerning the whereabouts of the bear, and three times she refused to tell him. But when he asked the fourth time she was compelled to tell him the place that he sought was near the high, sharp rocks which hurt the eyes of all who look at them. The next morning he went to this place and walked round and round the rocks. He did not meet the bear, and he did not come on any trail of him. But suddenly, looking up at the top of the rocks, he saw the bear's head sticking out. The bear was watching him. For Nayenezgáni was tracking the bear now, instead of the bear tracking him.

The bear's den was high up on the rocks in the shape of a cross.

It had four entrances. When Elder Brother looked into the eastern door he could not see the bear at all. Then he looked into the southern and western doors. He went this way in a sun circle until he came to the northern door, and there he saw the head of the crouching bear. But The-Bear-Who-Tracks-People saw Elder Brother first, and it ran away to the southern door and stuck its head out. Elder Brother had guessed that the bear would do this so he was there before the bear was, and he just cut the big head right off with his stone knife. Then he talked to the head of the bear. He said,

"Ho, ho, you were a bad one in your old life. You hurt many of my people. But in your new life you are going to be useful to them. You shall furnish them with rich food and sweet nuts. You shall give them white foam-fat with which to wash their bodies and strong thread to sew into their clothing." Then he cut the head into many pieces and threw them to the four corners of the world. They turned into yucca and mescal and many other useful plants. He cut off the nipples and threw them up into the sky where they turned into pinyon nuts on small sturdy trees. He cut off the left front paw to show as a trophy to his family. Then he went home to rest.

But soon he heard of the Traveling Stone called Tsenagáhi. It was to be found in the middle of a lake, and it had many strange powers. It could shoot off pieces of itself in the shape of arrows. It could turn itself into fire and other elements. It could scent the approach of people and turn itself into water before their eyes. He decided to test his strength against this stone. Why should a stone have so much power? His mother begged and begged him not to go. But the next morning, when the wind was blowing from the south side of the lake, he approached the home of the Traveling Stone from the north. He could find no trail of it, so he went east and south. Then the Stone smelled his coming. Before Elder Brother knew what was happening, the Stone had risen from the center of the waters and hurled itself at him. All that Elder Brother could do was to hold up his lightning arrow in its path.

This struck the Traveling Stone and split off many fragments from it. So the Stone knew that it had an enemy more powerful than itself, and it just kept right on rolling away. But wherever it went the young hero went too. He kept on shooting pieces from the sides of it, and soon there were great pieces of rock all over the country.

At a place where many trees ran down to the water the Traveling Stone slipped through into the river and sank down into the current of the stream. Elder Brother ran along the bank and tried to get ahead of it. He saw it gleaming through the waters, but it was always changing its position. Three times he headed it off, but the Stone only dipped more deeply into the stream bed. When he headed it off for the fourth time, he saw it shining like fire in the lowest level of the river, and he heard it speak to him.

"My baby hero, my darling son and grandson, go away and leave me alone, I beg of you. You do not know what you are doing. I am something of great value for your people. I will promise not to harm them any more if you will just leave me in my home under the waters. If you understand what I am you would not want to destroy me. I will hold the springs in the mountains open for you. I will keep all the rivers flowing. It will help The People if I do this. But if you kill me and splinter me all into nothingness your land will become forever barren."

The words of the Stone made Elder Brother think. He told it that he would spare it if it would always keep the waters in motion. And the Stone kept its promise, and later became the Water Monster of the upper world.

After this meeting with the Stone it was necessary for Elder Brother to rest for four days. He showed the trophies to The People and told them that very few of the monsters were alive. The twins knew that they had used up most of their strength and that before they followed any more of the evil ones they must go to the Sun Father again to ask for more of his power. On the morning of the fourth night after this period of rest in their mother's hogan they started toward the east. After a pleasant journey with no signs of enemy trails they entered the square turquoise house beside the wide eastern water where they had found their father. There they settled down on some red stone seats. They knew they must not sit on the white stone benches or on the turquoise benches because they were still making war against the monsters, and these white and blue benches were the seats on which to obtain peaceful strength.

When the Sun Bearer arrived he was tired. It was late afternoon, and there was a storm in the sky world. He sighed as he drew off the great shield of the sun and hung it on a peg in the wall. He lighted his turquoise pipe and stretched out to rest. He knew that the young heroes were there, but he did not pay any attention to them until he had eaten. Then he said,

"My children, why do you come again?"

"We come for no special purpose. We come just to see you and spend some time in your company."

Three times the Sun Bearer asked them why they had come, and three times they answered him in this way. The fourth time he said,

"My sons, now it is time for you to speak truly. When you came to see me on your first journey I gave you everything for which you asked. What more do you want?"

Then Younger Brother said, "Our father, we hear that a number of enemy monsters are still alive. We wish to know how to destroy them."

Sun Bearer said, "I helped you before even though some of the enemy monsters that you wished to kill were my children, too. At that time I asked for nothing in return. Now I am willing to help you again, but first I wish to know if you will do something for me. I have a long way to travel every day, and often, in the long summer days, I do not get through with my work on time. Then I have no place to rest or eat until I get back to this home of mine in the east. I wish you to ask the Turquoise Woman, your mother, if she is willing to make a home for me in the west, on an island by the great water."

"Yes, we will ask her," said Elder Brother. "But remember she is under the power of no one. She must speak for herself."

Then the Sun Bearer went behind each of the four curtains in the room in which they were. He brought out many presents for Estsánatlehi, their mother. He gave them shining hoops of different colors and stone knives and round, polished hailstones and jewels and many other valuable gifts from his hard goods and his soft goods.

As the brothers started out on their homeward journey they saw a great vision. Their father had taken them to the hole in the center of the sky world, and there The Gods spread before them the picture of the land of The People as it would be in the future when men increased in the land and became prosperous and happy.

They arrived at their home singing a song. After they had given their mother the gifts, she used them to make a great storm take place—for that had been the purpose of the Sun Bearer. He knew in this way that she had answered his question. The face of the land was changed. There were many new canyons and mountains with cloud flowers floating over them and rainbows spreading everywhere.

"Surely, now all the monsters are dead. The storm must have destroyed them," the Turquoise Woman said.

But the Spirit Wind was there and whispered again in the ears of her sons. There were still four evil ones left. These monster creatures and Enemy Gods were called Old Age Woman, Cold Woman, Poverty and Hunger.

Elder Brother asked his mother where to find Old Age Woman, but she would not answer him. Not until the fourth time would she tell him that she lived in the mountains near Depént-tsa. So when morning came Elder Brother started out for the northern mountains. After many days of wandering he saw an old woman who hobbled along on a staff. She was a very ancient creature for her hair was whiter than snow or cotton, her face was deeply lined, and her back was twisted over. Elder Brother said to her,

"My grandmother, I have bad news for you. I have come to kill you. You bring great trouble to The People, and we do not want you around any more. I am sorry my errand is so cruel a one."

"Why do you wish to kill me?" she asked in a weak voice. "I have never really hurt anyone. I know that you have done much to help your people, but I also help them in my own way. If you slay me, the numbers of The People will stand still. The older men will no longer give way to the boys. The boys will grow up to be fathers, and there will be no homes for them. Do you not know that it is well that old people should pass away in order to give their places to the young? Let me live, my grandson, and I will help you to increase the numbers of The People."

Elder Brother looked and looked at her. He decided that she was a very wise old woman, so he spared her life. He returned to his mother's house without a trophy.

The next day he sought for Cold Woman who lived on the highest summits of the mountains where the snow never melts. He climbed among peaks of the northern mountains where no tree grows and where the snow lies white and deep all through the summer. Here he found a thin, brown old woman sitting on the ice-covered ground. She had no shelter, no food, no fire and no warm clothing. Her teeth chattered, and she was shaking from head to foot and back again. Her eyes watered in drops which changed to icicles on her cheeks. The drifting snows blown by the northern blasts piled around her, and the only movement of life was in a flock of snow buntings which was flying and whirling around her. She had sent for them to foretell the coming of a great blizzard.

Elder Brother could hardly stand against the force of the wind and whirling snow. He drew his warm clothing tightly about him, and shouted to Cold Woman,

"Grandmother, I am very sorry indeed, but I have come to kill you. My People suffer from all the sickness you send them in the winter. Too many of them die because you send the cold winds and too much snow." Then he raised his stone knife to strike her.

Cold Woman said to the hero, with her teeth knocking together,

"You may kill me or not; do just whatever you must. It makes no difference to me. But if you kill me there will be no more snow and the springs will dry up. It will always be hot in your land. The waters will cease to flow. The People will die from heat and thirst. I think it will be better for them if you leave me alone."

So Elder Brother lowered his hand and thought a while. At last he said,

"My grandmother, your words are true."

Then he turned around and went home again without a thing to show for his journey.

When the Spirit Wind whispered that Poverty still lived he asked his mother again to direct him. When she would not do so the Spirit Wind told him. There were two of them, an old man and an old woman who lived near Waterless Mountain. When he arrived there next day he found an old woman and an old man in dirty, torn clothing. They were very dirty, indeed, and they owned no hard goods and no soft goods. Their hogan was very bare with no firewood near by. He said to them,

"Grandmother and grandfather, I am sorry to be so cruel to you. I have come to kill you for the sake of The People."

"Our grandchild," the old man said, "it would not be wise to kill us. In the time to come your people would miss us. They would never have any new clothes and would have to live in such rags as you see on us. If we live, their clothing will wear out, and The People will have to make many new and beautiful garments. They will gather many hard goods and soft goods because they will have to work. They will be strong and handsome in their new buckskin garments. Let us live, so that we can pull their old clothes into rags for them. You will see that we are necessary."

So Elder Brother agreed and went home again, thinking. And he had no trophy this time, either.

But Hunger was still living, so the Spirit Wind told him where to find him. It was at a place where there was a large spot covered with white grass. And here he found not one but twelve Hunger People. They had a head man who was very fat even though he had only little brown cactus plants for his food. Elder Brother said to him,

"I want you to know why I have come to kill you and your people. It is necessary for me to be cruel so that men may suffer no more from the pain of hunger, so that they will die no more from starving."

"It would be very foolish of you to kill us. We are really friends of yours. If we die The People will no longer enjoy their food. If you want your people to increase in the days to come you must let us live. If we go men and women will not know the pleasure which comes from the cooking pot and the eating of all good things. They will not enjoy the stilling of their hungers and the quieting of their thirsts. And they will never care to go hunting and know all the rewards it brings."

So Elder Brother changed his mind again and went home very slowly, thinking, as he climbed down the mountainside. Perhaps some of the enemy monsters were necessary for The People. These last ones seemed to be, anyway. When he arrived at his mother's house, he took off all his flint armor and laid down all of his weapons. He put all of his buckskin garments into a pile with his knives and arrows. He said to his mother,

"As I came along everyone spoke to me as to a relative. Each one called me 'son' or 'brother' or 'grandson.' I think all the enemy monsters must be dead." And he sang a song after this. His younger brother was very glad to see him, and they sat and smoked in peace and in silence. Their mother, the Turquoise Woman, was very happy to have them there in her hogan, so she cooked for them all the food they liked to eat, and as she cooked she sang a song about the meat and the corn.

A PSYCHOLOGICAL
COMMENTARY

By JOSEPH L. HENDERSON

THIS COLLECTION of Navajo stories speaks clearly of the
history and character of a people who inhabit a broad area of
mountainous desert in northern Arizona and New Mexico, the
modern descendants of an ancient people who at one time wandered
freely over our continent but are now caught, and so to speak en-
cysted, within our American culture. Limited as they are to a
definite though spacious area, The People, as they proudly call
themselves, are nevertheless surprisingly unlimited culturally, and
true to their native mode of life. They live in small family groups
peaceably as sheepherders, silversmiths, weavers, and farmers, yet
they are under no illusion that they inhabit some arcadian paradise.
They are realistic, individualistic, curious and wary, but they also
have a large and unique talent for enacting religious ceremonials
and for practicing the arts of healing.

   The story of *The Beggar Wanderer* describes one of the ways
in which the Navajo thinks of himself, as a wanderer and a beggar
not unlike the great nomads of antiquity who sought and never truly
found the promised land. It is a sad story, with its compensatory
wish for property and a place in the sun. Another story, *In the Garden of the Home God*, tells of the joys of a settled life for which
the wandering Navajo searched and which he presumably found
in the valleys of New Mexico. The Navajos may have been
originally a nomadic people: in any event, certain anthropological

evidence, of which Sapir's is a linguistic example,[1] supports the assumption that the Navajos journeyed to their present habitat from the northwestern plains. There is at least one story the Navajos have in common with the plains tribes, the story of the Changing Coyote, a sort of renegade or outlaw symbolizing all that is untamable in man, and perhaps standing for the restlessness peculiar to a nomadic people as opposed to the necessary immobility of an agricultural people. Coyote is sometimes a man, sometimes a god, sometimes an animal; a restless trickster, inquisitive, obscene, adventurous and diabolically challenging—a desert Mephistopheles. It was Coyote who first recognized death as a necessary evil and who during the creation impatiently hurled the stars into the sky, refusing to wait until they could be placed there in an orderly fashion. It is also related that he stole fire from the gods, that he seduced the sister of eleven holy youths by witchcraft and changed her into a bear, not to speak of less sinister and more mundane seductions in his role as "a very well-dressed man." Coyote is sometimes the Devil, sometimes Prometheus, sometimes Dionysus, sometimes Don Juan, but mostly just a plain nuisance.

At the opposite pole from Coyote are the Holy Ones, beneficent Navajo gods who care for The People by some celestial dispensation of law and order. The story of *The Dreamer* relates in a deeply moving spirit how the Navajo medicine man contacts these gods, the Yei, in order not only to procure their helpful cooperation in sending rain to the desert but to transmit from them to The People the immortal ceremonials and songs. From the Yei, above all, they obtain the healing strength of the designs known as sand or pollen paintings which are made for every great occasion of tribal life, especially as medicine for curing sick bodies and souls. Most of the Yei stand aloof from the affairs of every day, and their ministrations are made available solely through the medicine man; but there is one god who is clearly patterned after every typical mother's father or brother, a kindly, humorous, stern, wise and ubiquitous uncle named Talking God. It is Talking God

[1] References will be found on page 140.

who imparts the knowledge of tribal customs, with their strict adherence to the right way of ordering interpersonal relationships, property, sex, marriage and obedience to the family hierarchy. Therefore, he is the guardian of the tribal culture pattern.

Then there are the Twins or Warrior Gods, well-known figures which the Navajos have in common with world mythology. (The twin heroes are known in the Babylonian, Grecian, Roman, Japanese and Polynesian cultures.) The Navajo Twins follow the pattern of these other hero figures, while maintaining local characteristics. The story relates that Changing Woman is impregnated by the Sun and brings forth the Twins. They are reared in the mother's residence until at a precocious age they leave home and find their way through many trials of strength to the Sun's house, where they are at first rejected, then tested, then initiated as sons of the father. Finally they are armed as warriors by their father and sent forth to overcome the monsters. Since the myth of the Twins cannot be correlated with any specific Navajo culture pattern, we are obliged to look for a historical-psychological meaning deeper and broader than the one supplied by cultural anthropology. Not only the Twins but also Coyote and the Yei exhibit qualities which can only be understood as parts of a universal myth.[2]

The main task of this commentary is to analyze the parts of the universal myth shown in these stories. First, however, I should like to digress for a moment in order to show the reader how he may best enjoy reading them. The Navajo stories have the character of folk tales, by which we mean that local features (usually animal, plant and climatic conditions peculiar to the region) are freely woven into the texture of the otherwise timeless myths. Some readers may enjoy this local storytellers' art and be content to ignore deeper meanings. There is a good deal to be said for this approach. Mrs. Link relates in her preface how she received much of her material in this way, from Navajos who told her stories while she sat and knitted. Whatever the reader's main interest in the myths, he should read them over two and three times so that the storyteller's magic has a chance to pierce the shell of his over-sophisticated taste, and touch the heart. A first reading of one of these stories is almost certain to convey an impression of naïveté, and the modern reader is likely to adopt an indulgent attitude as one might to the storytelling of a child. But if he persists in his reading, taking note of every small detail of the narrative, this illusion will, I think, be dispelled. Then the Navajo storyteller will reveal himself as an extremely knowledgeable recorder of sensory impressions and psychological facts. Unknown to himself, he occasionally combines the observation of a natural scientist and the insight of a poet into a kind of radiant natural humanism.

A good example of this kind of description is found in the passage where He-Who-Teaches-Himself mourns the personal loss of his pet turkey, yet consecrates the species to the usefulness of the tribe. "From his turkey were descended all the turkeys that are tame in the world today. And all the beautiful things the man saw in his pet turkey are still to be seen in all the turkeys that live today. In its feathers are the colors of the corn and the shining black of the rain cloud. The flash of lightning and the gleam of the rainbow can be seen on its plumes when it walks in the sunlight. The darkness of rain is in its beard, and it carries the sign of the blue bean on its forehead."

In the antics of Coyote there is a Disneyesque play of phantasy ranging from impish gaiety to sadistic fury, and these episodes are told with just that sobering fear of the irresponsible in human behavior mixed with the sense of release that a man feels who is able to laugh at himself at his worst.

If it were only a question of literary enjoyment, however, these stories could not hold their own with the richly varied folklore of Asia and Europe. But here their simplicity gives them a strength not commonly found in more consciously elaborated tales. Behind the delicate perception of natural phenomena, the Navajo is a natural psychologist showing his awareness of inner psychic facts. He describes the arduous journeys of his heroes over mountains and deserts which imperceptibly lose their outer reality and become, as it were, landscapes of human emotion reaching heights of elation and depths of despair. The journey itself becomes a journey of inner exploration in which a man, at variance with the contrasting opposites in his nature, strains toward a goal of unity expressed paradoxically as a fourfold symbol of wholeness. The psychologist can find in these stories a sure intuition of the same symbolism Jung has demonstrated in the dream material of highly complex modern men and women, studied by recently fashioned concepts of analytical psychology. This parallel is strikingly illustrated in the story where He-Who-Teaches-Himself goes to a place where male and female rivers cross (point of greatest conflict). He is whirled about four times on a raft (reorientation to the idea of unity) to reach a center (symbol of the Self) by which the gods initiate him and thereby change him into a different sort of person, He-Who-Floats-Upon-The-Waters (attainment of psychological consciousness over and above the unconscious).

Such a striking parallel between a simple folk tale and a complex psychological theory is apt to raise a host of questions which cannot be answered in a brief commentary; I will attempt, however, to answer the simplest of them. Let us start with the conscious and the unconscious. In terms of the conscious mind human nature in a worldly sense does not change. In fact most people are so like themselves (expansive or withdrawn, cold or impassioned) as to become almost museum pieces of all that personality and environment have made them. If, however, we look into the depths of what has been unconscious, we see a totally different picture, the picture that the Navajo storyteller sees when he implies that the whole point of the mythic process is change and only change. Coyote changes from white to yellow; the Twins change from two to four; He-Who-Teaches-Himself changes utterly, as I have indicated.

Freud had some inkling of these mythical psychic depths when he described the existence of impulses for life (pleasure principle) and impulses for self-destruction (death wish). Exploring this *terra incognita* more deeply still, Jung was able to affirm the existence of a common substratum of psychic imagery (archetypes) charged with psychic energy existing in a primordial form. In recent years this research has blossomed into a method for studying the data of mythology without doing violence to its original meaning.[3] By elucidating each "mythologem" (i.e., myth cycle) which comprises the universal myth, Jung has been able to show how it may be used to understand:

1. The mythologem of the culture pattern as a whole or its various elements.

2. An historical period within a particular culture.

3. An individual's experience of such a mythologem in the context of a particular period within his culture.

This is a new application of the older theories of Jung which originally replaced the over-personal, "reductive" method of Freud and his followers. The results of Jung's earlier research established that all mythological manifestations of the unconscious, whether appearing in the dreams or phantasies of individuals or in the myths of large groups of people, can be traced to a "collective unconscious" where psychic energy exists in its primordial form. Jung further described this energy as appearing primarily in the form of archaic images, later becoming differentiated as an individual grows out of his childhood identification with his parents or a group grows out of its identification with obsolete primitive culture patterns. The energy thus activated is never finite and therefore never perishable, nor is it either good or bad from a conscious point of view. It is essentially amoral and immortal, being always capable of renewal in an autonomous manner. Yet it is purposive also. It is therefore life-promoting and life-inhibiting but never nihilistic; at its source it is essentially dual, though not in conflict, and it is impartial in promoting the favorable and the unfavorable in human life.

I shall try to demonstrate the applicability of this method in relation to the hero cycles of the Navajo stories.

The applicability of this theory of psychic energy to the Coyote myths is particularly striking. Like Jung's psychic energy, Coyote is irrepressible and immortal, his life being kept in the tip of his nose and the tip of his tail. It is related that the Bear Maiden, in trying to get rid of her unwelcome lover, "crushed him into little bits and three times he was reborn. The fourth time she worked so hard to destroy him that she practically ground him to powder as she would corn, but she didn't hurt the tip of his tail and nose." His primordial nature is emphasized in *The First Worlds and the Flood*, where he provokes a flood by stealing the children of the Water Monster. Though he is the satanic betrayer of The People in this episode, he is also in a way their saviour, for it is he who, by ascending a hollow reed along with other animals, makes a way for all to ascend from a lower to a higher world.

Coyote, then, is a personification of the demonic aspect of life at a primordial level. It is interesting in this connection that Paul Radin, in attempting to correlate anthropological and psychological data, speaks of the Coyote stories in general as representing the most primitive form of hero myth, a form for which a Jungian explanation is preferable to the Freudian, namely that Coyote is a symbol for undifferentiated libido corresponding to a "primordial" level of primitive culture.[4]

We will now go on to determine the specific mythologem which Coyote represents for the Navajos. The Navajo Coyote legends, as I suggested earlier, bear a strong compensatory relation to the tribal laws and peaceful customs dispensed by Talking God. Coyote is therefore more than a reflection of the primordial unconscious; he is also a dynamic personality at odds with the ideal of tribal conformity. (Primitive people are in fact compulsively careful in their conformity to custom.)

Jung has described this type of semipersonalized figure standing in contrast to the Persona in individual psychology as the Shadow.[5] Although we are dealing with collective psychology and not individual psychology, we can nevertheless apply this concept to the coyote figure by postulating a tribal group-consciousness (expressed as manifest culture pattern), analogous to ego-consciousness in an individual. Hence the culture pattern of the tribe, like the ego-consciousness of the individual, may be expected to exhibit its appropriate Shadow counterpart. Let us see if the Navajo stories bear this out.

The nature of the Navajo gods, the ceremonials supposed to have been imparted by them to the medicine man, the meticulous order in which the songs are sung and the sand paintings executed are related in the story of *The Dreamer*. We learn here of the Navajo ideal of right behavior in an ordered society, a society which considers that its health comes from establishing a perfectly harmonious relation (1) to the cosmos, and (2) to a family in which a man's father is his mother's father or brother, and in which he is expected to obey a strict code of exogamy enforced by powerful beneficent mothers, the culture being matrilinear. If, as I say, we bear in mind all these factors at once, whether real or ideational in Navajo life, we could hardly invent a more suitable personification for the Shadow side of such a culture pattern than Coyote.

If we look more closely at this conception of the Shadow as represented in individual psychology, we find two different aspects of this figure, described by Jung as *personal* and *impersonal*. The personal aspect of the Shadow is that spirit of perversity which tempts a child (or an adult) to behave directly contrary to his ego-ideal. The impersonal aspect of the Shadow is the archetypal aspect which appears in dreams or phantasies as a devilish or witch-like figure. Jung writes of it as follows: "One of the dominants which is almost always met with in analysis of projections of the collective unconscious contents is a magical demon of preponderating sinister effect. . . ." Coyote as a sneak thief and lecherous buffoon is an all too human (i.e., personalized) Shadow figure, caricaturing a man's best idea of himself as a law-abiding citizen, but in that truly frightening story *The Woman Who Became a Bear*, Coyote is a very different figure, indeed a magical demon creating a "preponderating sinister effect[6] of the archetypal Shadow, who embodies all that the Navajos consider most deeply sinful and of which they are deeply afraid, namely witchcraft, incest and death."[7]

In the study of the Shadow as a special obstruction to psychic health, one all-important consideration must be emphasized. While the Shadow seems to present only the vilest features of a man's behavior pattern, it nonetheless contains one feature which he desperately needs and must possess if he is to become whole. For everyone this feature seems unique, depending upon the nature of his own personal problem. But if we could abstract from all the individual Shadows the virtue covered with this black cloak, it would, I think, approximate the Navajo conception of the White Coyote in his symbolic personification of mobility, spontaneity and curiosity combined with an inner sense of rightness which stumbles upon good as well as bad, a creative experimentalism that is essential to man's capacity for self-renewal. Coyote possesses in a primitive form a trait common to all archetypal Shadow figures, the unexpected promise of redemption. Like Goethe's Mephistopheles, he is "part of that power which seeking evil finds the good," or like the *golem* of the Jewish legend (described by Meyrink in *Der Golem*), a sinister automaton through whom nevertheless the whole ancestral past may be redeemed.

This being so, Coyote may represent a still more inclusive archetype. In a recent monograph on the figure of Mercurius, the central figure of Hermetic philosophy, Jung has described a trickster embodying a special notion of the paradoxical in human nature; and this figure, which includes and transcends his previous conception of the Shadow, is strikingly like Coyote. Although Coyote is not the divine *artifex* of alchemy in its developed form, still he seems to be its primitive counterpart. Like Mercurius he "consists of all conceivable opposites. He is therefore definitely a duality which, however, is spoken of as a unity, in spite of the fact that its many inner contradictions can separate dramatically into an equal number of disparate and apparently independent figures." He is also "material and spiritual." He is "the process by which the lower material is transformed into the higher and spiritual and vice versa." He is "The devil, a redeemer pointing the way, an evasive trickster and the reflection of the godhead in material nature."[8]

At bottom then we have in Coyote an embodiment of that creative experimentalism in man which corresponds to the trickster archetype: we never know how it is going to act, even when we think we know. I cannot think of a better example of Coyote psychology in our own time than the predicament of modern statesmen who sanction the stockpiling of atomic weapons for the destruction of future enemies, while at the same time they promise to suppress atomic energy for warlike purposes and convert it to the uses of peace. These perfectly well-meaning statesmen, who in fact are ourselves, do not appear to find any inconsistency in this attitude, which nonetheless represents a basic split between the destructive and creative principles of life. We simply do what seems most effective at the time.

Let us turn now to the mythologem represented by the Twins. The lack of culture or group identity in a primitive culture makes for interpersonal suspiciousness, shiftless behavior and general demoralization on the part of most of the primitive group's members. This has its counterpart in our adolescents before role-diffusion[9] is replaced by ego-identity. Therefore, if in one of his aspects Coyote represents a kind of juvenile delinquency, the Twins represent the achievement of identity within the tribal culture pattern.

This identity is first of all aware of its double nature. Unlike Coyote, whose duality of being is fortuitous and unconscious of itself, the Twins are consciously linked together, two sons each seeking the same father. They are both Ego and Shadow aspects of each other, representing introverted and extroverted polarities, but they live in symbiotic harmony. One is active and dominating, the other reflective and reactive; together they form an interactive combination of traits basic to all character formation in an individual sense. But to begin with, they are young, and to that extent undifferentiated. In the series of pollen paintings reproduced in *Where the Two Came to Their Father*,[10] the Twins are first represented as both black (i.e., identical and unconscious); then one is represented as black and the other blue, depicting their separate and contrasting natures. In these phases they are as yet uninitiated, which means that they are still not fully differentiated.

Jung is the modern psychologist who first hit upon the age-old problem of character differentiation,[11] and he arrived at the hypothesis of two contrasting types, the extrovert and the introvert. He was not satisfied by the simplicity of this conception, although at first it seemed to explain all major difference in human character. At length he described four character traits,[12] or four functions which supplement and finally differentiate the original duality of human nature. Significantly, the Navajo Twins who, after becoming differentiated into their original introvert-extrovert duality, after their encounter with the Sun Father as initiating agent immediately became four, as being more appropriate to their higher differentiation.

There is an interesting and important story to tell of the way in which this transition from two to four is made possible, one that cannot be told in detail in this short commentary. It concerns the archetype of initiation which asserts itself at a crucial point in adolescent development, changing the boy into a man by bringing to him personally a new evaluation of ego-identity, and representing historically the classical surrender of the individual to the accepted tribal discipline. It is the "rite" of initiation with its purification, its trials of strength and its aspiration toward the highest human development conceivable to the earliest culture-conscious men.

Culture, however, in this sense is still a collective phenomenon, and for all its great advantage over a primordial unconsciousness, may stimulate men to overreach themselves in a quest for power. The Twins in our story do succumb to this type of ego inflation. Accordingly after their initiation they set forth upon their supreme adventure of overcoming monsters, an easy task for them with their newly acquired weapons, but once started they do not know how or where to stop. Most heroes finally die as the victims of their own power drive, but the Navajos have conceived a more humane and more psychologically plausible solution. When the Twins return to the earth from their adventures in skyland, they are taken in hand by Talking God, that most human deity, who reminds them to cool their blood and learn the arts of peace in tribal life.[13] More than this, one gathers that some sweet dispensation of their inward natures teaches them ultimately to transcend even tribal and cultural conformity. It is said that they grew sick from their longing to overcome still other lesser monsters, and had to heal themselves by their own songs.

In this connection we may think again of our modern condition. One could wish that our statesmen, who are (as I have suggested) also ourselves in a certain respect, would heed the wisdom of Talking God and advise the warrior gods to drop their quest for power. Having overcome the Nazis, we should at least not delude ourselves that overcoming the Communists will make an end of war. Besides the great monsters there will always be other lesser monsters to conquer until we learn to live peaceably with ourselves, and to heal our sickness with our own songs.

The final apotheosis of the Twins represents them in the pollen painting as four figures, each standing upon a separate mountain, each with an arc of rainbow over his head, perfectly balanced and at rest between earth and sky, symmetrical and ordered to the last degree of perfection in this medium. In the same way Jung has described the coming into being of the sense of wholeness and balance that characterizes the mature person at the goal of his journey out of original chaos, out of childhood, out of collective identification—the characteristics of a being who is related to all he has known and experienced of the world, but who has won the essential crown of consciousness over and above it all. Probably it is only the medicine man in a tribal society who can apprehend the nature of this process by which a man becomes an individual beyond collective adaptation, and even he may be more the victim of such knowledge than its master; what is certain is that he is its mouthpiece. Mrs. Link has given us a very good picture of the Navajo medicine man: "In the terms of analytical psychology the medicine man is an introverted intuitive type. Reaching into his inner depths in concentrated periods of creative introversion, he has discovered the forms of the collective images. Today we know that the dominating ideas of the unconscious mind are peculiarly accessible to this type of human being . . ."[14]

The medicine man's vocation, which consists in his ability to expose his own psyche to the imprint of archetypes, is beautifully told in *The Dreamer*, which I have previously mentioned. More important to our present concern is the story of another prototype of the medicine man, *He-Who-Teaches-Himself*, which expresses the claim of an individual to submit to a process of initiation totally different from the tribal initiation. With the help of the gods, He-Who-Teaches-Himself seals himself in a hollow log and floats down a river "to an underground lake which lay below the meeting place of the rivers. . . ." After an encounter with the Water Monster from which he is rescued by the God of Fire, he comes to a whirlpool or whirling lake, from which he is saved and becomes the twice-named. Thenceforth he discovers the woman who is to represent his share of the eternal feminine (i.e., anima) and has to free her from the evil influence of her father, Deer Raiser, who personifies the Shadow. In her interpretation, Mrs. Link makes it clear that the determination of He-Who-Teaches-Himself to undertake such a journey represents the need of an individual to disidentify with the collective norm, to find the depths of his own nature in a journey which carries him through typical dangers, to reach a center which can never be related directly to the outer tasks or satisfactions of life. Mrs. Link describes this center as the "place of ritual birth in which he is tossed about four times before he can reach the center. Two crossed log rafts are whirled about this lake of the spirit. The hero is supposed to be enclosed in one of them. Yet it seems as though two aspects of him are joined together at this time of testing . . . A great tossing and churning in the basin of the circular lake is caused by the gods kneeling at the four ends of the logs." This reminds us of the caldron of ancient Irish mythology in which various parts of the hero were "cooked" together in a ritual ceremony in order to make a complete assimilation of all the parts of his nature. He-Who-Teaches-Himself, then, approaches the center in himself which Jung has described as the goal of the psychological individuation process. In the end he "returns to his family and teaches his younger brother the details of the new ceremony, the Feather Chant. The younger brother represents the earthly counterpart of himself [who] can assume the tribal duties of the medicine man and preserve the necessary knowledge for his people. . . . The Self Teacher and new man is free now to live his own life, to return to his mate and his farm."[15]

In the stories of these three hero cycles represented by Coyote, the Twins and He-Who-Teaches-Himself, we may perhaps perceive three basic mythologems—three stages in the development both of early culture and of all those of us who have the psychological task of coming to terms with our own primitive conflicts in order to reach a better degree of self-understanding. I can best compare these mythologems by singling out the archetype they all share in common, namely the theme of the Journey.[16]

Coyote is the one who "just keeps traveling along" whether upon the white trail of virtue or the yellow trail of evil. He is always two and has no goal, our beggar wanderer and trickster. The Twins have found another direction and pursue a different though still dual journey, first along the rainbow path of adventure and then along the pollen path of peace. For them there is a sequence: first a beginning at their place of origin, then a transition from below upward to sky and back to earth, and finally an end firmly rooted in cosmic space. As I have indicated, this mythologem corresponds to the archetype of initiation, followed by the growing security of the ego learning to live in harmony with the existing culture pattern of a settled people, a people who have given up or are trying to give up their nomadic and/or warlike ways. The journey of He-Who-Teaches-Himself is from the beginning individual, unified and nonheroic in the outer sense, yet deeply heroic in the inner spiritual sense. It is the mythologem of an inner journey, or journey of the soul, which embodies the awareness of the Self in a person who has learned to transcend the limits of ego-consciousness.

In the stories of this collection there are other allusions to the archetype of the Journey. In *The First Worlds and the Flood* the first people ascend from the lowest levels of the underworld through a hollow reed; the tentative beginnings of consciousness and the impulse toward differentiation are indicated by the necessity of reaching each time a new level to escape the flood which would otherwise engulf them in a retrogressive return to the deep unconscious of preculture. In another story, *The River of Separation*, we have a tragic picture of man's failure to preserve the right balance of the male and female elements, ostensibly in his relationships but more deeply within himself, so that the river, which should be the River of Life, on whose broad current all should travel to a goal of cultural integration, becomes instead the River of Separation which divides men from women and man from his own soul. Whether vertical or horizontal, in parabola or spiral or circle, the other journeys display themselves as ways of change making available to consciousness the precious differences which define each stage of psychic development.

These journeys have not one but many goals, and these are hard to define, especially in language. The Navajos represent them as they have always been represented in the great religious systems of antiquity (which no doubt the Navajos have inherited from their Asian ancestors, and mixed with their dreams out of the primordial unconscious in sun-baked New Mexico), as a four-square field embracing or embraced by a circle, forming the image of an inner world within an outer world. In the beautiful simplicity of the Navajo sand painting, this eternally original design conveys the idea of a periodic state of psychic unity won from conflict at the nodal points of life where one journey ends and another is about to begin.

[1] Edward Sapir, *Collected Works*, University of California Press, 1951.

[2] See Joseph Campbell, *The Hero with a Thousand Faces*, Bollingen-Pantheon, 1949.

[3] See C. G. Jung and Carl Kerenyi, *Essays on a Science of Mythology*, Bollingen-Pantheon, 1949.

[4] Paul Radin, *Hero Cycles of the Winnebago Indians*, Indiana University Press, 1949.

[5] H. G. Baynes, elaborating the Jungian concept of the Shadow, describes it as a "renegade tendency" or "renegade hypothesis" which delights in disobeying all moral pressure, even to the point of ensuring the renegade's own undoing or destruction. H. G. Baynes, *Mythology of the Soul*, Williams & Wilkins (Baltimore), 1946.

[6] C. G. Jung, "Psychology of Unconscious Processes," *Collected Papers* (edited by Constance Long), Balliere, Tindall Cox (London), 1920, p. 433.

[7] See Clyde Kluckhohn and Dorothea Leighton, *The Navaho*, Harvard University Press, 1946.

[8] C. G. Jung, *The Spirit Mercury*, Analytical Psychology Club of New York Publications, 1953, p. 35.

[9] See E. H. Erickson, *Childhood and Society*, Norton, 1950. The expression *role-diffusion* refers to the many partial identifications an adolescent makes before he has achieved ego-identity or group-identity.

[10] By Maud Oakes (commentary by Joseph Campbell), Bollingen-Pantheon, 1943.

[11] See *Psychological Types*, Harcourt, Brace, 1924.

[12] Further evidence of the fourness of the Twins is found: "Among the Greeks, the Twins were denominated *anakes* . . . and sometimes instead of two the *anakes* were invoked as four . . ." Harold Bayley, *The Lost Language of Symbolism*, Williams & Norgate (London), 1912, p. 14.

[13] Joseph Campbell, commentary in *Where the Two Came to Their Father*, by Maud Oakes, Bollingen-Pantheon, 1943.

[14] Margaret Erwin Schevill (Link), *Beautiful on the Earth*, Hazel Dreis Editions (Santa Fe, New Mexico), 1947, p. 114.

[15] *Ibid.*, p. 148.

[16] As a psychotherapist, I can vouch for the very frequent occurrence of this theme in modern dreams. Its ubiquity in mythology is well known.

ẴPPENDIX

THE WAY IT BEGAN

It was 1925. The professor of Italian Language and Literature at the University of California had a friend visiting him, a businessman from the firm which outfitted trading posts on the Indian reservations of New Mexico and Arizona. This man spoke enthusiastically about the snake ceremonies of the Hopis as I sat beside him one night at dinner. Something like a Greek daemon spoke in me, and, before I knew it, I was planning to go to Arizona the following August.

My goal was to be the little Hopi town of Oraibi in northern Arizona. Letters had been written for me to various trading posts on the way. My husband urged me to go, and a friend volunteered to stay with the children. I packed some riding clothes in an old suitcase and took my sleeping bag.

It had been arranged with a trader at Sunrise Point, near Leupp, Arizona, that he should tell the mail carrier to pick me up at Canyon Diablo with the mail. But it turned out that the train on which I was did not stop at Canyon Diablo—that great cut in the earth of northern Arizona over which the trains crawl on a slender trestle. For a few minutes it looked as though I would have to go on to Flagstaff and disrupt my happily made plans. But the conductor relented, after much pleading on my part, to the extent of slowing the train, and I landed in the middle of the desert, which I had come to think of as containing great mysteries.

A very old Ford furnishes the best means of introduction to far-lying villages in Mexico or Ireland or Arizona, I have found. One's safety seems almost in inverse ratio to the dilapidation of its fenders and other parts. But "it takes you there; it brings you home again." So just at nightfall, through a sunset of incredible colors raying over the desert world, we crossed the bridge over the wash and arrived at Sunrise Point.

I saw the first Navajos in Nevy Smith's post. Nevy Smith is dead now. But on that evening long ago he stood hale and hearty and welcoming behind the counter in his trading post weighing out sugar for a Navajo woman who was dressed in a purple velveteen blouse and a long, green sateen skirt. Certain moments seem to be drawn like places on the map of memory, and this was one of them. This kindly trader to the Hopis and Navajos welcomed me with a flourish of the sugar scoop as he said everything in the post was at my service.

Soft, brown eyes in dark faces looked out of the half-light in the big, old stone building. Very tall men who looked like Tibetans in fur caps and colored headbands stared at me. Little children peeked out from all the angles of their mothers' voluminous skirts. The sugar was exchanged for a rug of intricate, conventional design. Some canned fruit was acquired in place of a sheep's pelt. Nevy Smith gave the children bags of candy.

My room was an enclosure of hanging blankets in one corner of the building. In the large, dark space where I was surrounded by piles of saddles and rugs, by sacks of aromatic coffee and shelves of pottery, I went to sleep in the middle of a large brass bedstead, snug in my own sleeping bag.

In the morning at the one small window Navajo faces pressed against the panes. White women were rare visitors in those days on the reservation. But why was the "bellicana" going to a Hopi snake dance? Of course, they were going, too, but there were better things to see. I was yet to learn of the feeling between the Navajos and the Hopis—traditional and necessary enemies—or of the wonderful Navajo chants.

At an early hour we were on our way to Oraibi and Lorenzo Hubbell. At Red Lake the road had to take a wide detour because the summer rains had inundated the old basin. We ate our lunch of sardines and crackers and oranges in a little arroyo of rose-colored earth. Enormous rocky formations of butte and mesa stood out on the horizon. We passed drifting flocks of sheep with Navajo children herding them. The keen air grew lighter and more invigorating as we climbed through foothills and canyons.

We arrived in Oraibi and were the recipients of the hospitality of Lorenzo Hubbell. I had heard of his exquisite courtesy and politeness of the heart. But I was not prepared for the warm charm and generosity with which he treated truck drivers, mail carriers, artists, the governor of Arizona, and me. At his home, connected with the trading post, he was the center of life in that desert world for many different kinds of human beings. As I sat in his little parlor, decorated with the basket plaques of the Hopi and the rugs of the Navajo, I saw cowboys, Mormon farmers, mining engineers, government erosion experts, Navajo medicine men, Roman Catholic priests, Mennonite missionaries, and tourists of all descriptions passing through Oraibi.

Credit for a box of food for a sick Hopi child, his car to take an old, paralyzed Navajo woman to the Agency Hospital thirty-two miles away at Keam's Canyon, time to smoke a good cigar with a trader who had driven many miles to ask his advice—these represented only a few aspects of this many-sided man. In this lonely post, seventy-five miles from the railroad, he was carrying on the traditions of his Spanish ancestry.

Walpi, that high, sentinel town of the Hopis, to which we were going, was only a few miles beyond Oraibi. But it was a dramatic ride—then as it is now. We were just able to pull through the erratic and picturesque Oraibi wash. Around barriers of strangely shaped rock, coasting into canyons and out again with radiator boiling, we sped past Chimopavi and Polacca to glimpse Walpi ahead of us like an ancient temple high against the sky. At the foot of the trail up to the village a Navajo offered me his pony to ride. A steep path led us to a cluster of adobe houses around a plaza.

Just as the last rays of the sun spread out over the desert below we heard the sound of the bull-roarer in the hands of the antelope priests and saw the snake men with blackened faces dance with the bull snakes and diamond-backed rattlers in their mouths. Around and around in a circle in the little plaza they went. I could not realize what they were doing.

The spectator is allowed to see only the last forty minutes of this ceremony, which takes place at the end of nine days of ritual celebration. I knew the rite was a long prayer for rain, that most important element of desert life. I saw the serpents released to the four directions to take the prayers of the Hopi to the rain gods. The snakes were supposed to be the earthly brothers of the lightning which precedes the storm.

I stood behind the statuesque Hopi women who held the baskets of sacred corn meal which was to be sprinkled on the snakes. I saw a dancer bitten in the cheek and neck by a coiling snake which had not been subdued by the feather tickling of his attendant. Nothing happened. The man went on dancing. The drums were beating. A rhythmic, singing prayer went on and on.

Then suddenly it began to rain. I had never known anything like the feeling of communal happiness that spread around that high Hopi plaza.

That night at dinner Lorenzo entertained Governor Hunt and his party of visiting ethnologists, also just back from the Snake Dance. At his extended dining-table we ate roast lamb, fresh corn and peach pie. The largest coffee-pot I have ever seen circulated freely. There was an exchange of good talk and reminiscences.

The ethnologists were much interested in the differences between the Navajos and Hopis. Thy spoke of "acculturation patterns." One of them expressed amazement at the adaptability of the Navajos. He said he could not understand how a comparatively simple people, such as they were supposed to have been, could have become so proficient in many arts in so short a time.

He described their ingenuity in taking up weaving when they came in contact with it among the Hopis after the Spaniards had introduced wool into the southwest, and their superb accomplishment in a short time, in the working and designing of silver. That was all very well, Lorenzo said, but surely they must have brought some ability with them. Whatever they borrowed from other peoples they seemed to develop to a point beyond the original achievement.

They spoke of the Navajos as Athapascans, since they used a dialect of that language, as did the Apaches. There were supposed to be over fifty thousand of them.

The Navajos spoke of themselves as The Dinné, The People. They had been called "Navajos" by the Pueblo peoples. The Spaniards, on entering Arizona and New Mexico, had written of them as "Apaches de Navajo." Near the large pueblo ruin of Puyé there had been a smaller ruin known to the Tewas as "Navahu'u." An identity between this word, meaning "planted fields," and the word which Benavides used was suggested.

There was no doubt about the fact that they were the newest comers to the southwestern desert. The time of their living there seemed to be thought of as between five hundred and two thousand years. Of an Asiatic origin, they were supposed to have migrated slowly from the coasts of Alaska and through the forests of western Canada.

When Lorenzo spoke of the Navajo chants which were given in the late autumn, I hoped that I might see one of them someday. Reading my desire, he told me that it could be arranged whenever I could come.

As he drove me the next day to Leupp for a lunch at the Indian School, he told me many things about The People. He said that their religion was an attempt to get into touch with the powers of nature, to learn how to be in harmony with them. They knew the destructive forces—such as the terrible summer lightning-storms—but they had worked out a system of appeasing the powers behind them by proper attention. They thought that they could control a power which they knew about and to which they paid the right sacrifices. Of course, there were good and evil forces, but the only things which were really evil were the ones they did not know. So they personified everything which lived and moved in order to know about it and to learn to control it.

Lorenzo said there was an underlying belief in unity in all that the Navajos thought and did, but it was based, curiously, on a doubleness. Two elements had to come together to make a whole, two entirely different, opposite things such as light and darkness. Even the hogans which we were passing were of two types—male and female forms. The hogans, or Navajo houses, were largely circular in form and were supposed to represent the form of the universe, with the fire built always in the center.

The eastern part of the reservation was the male half, the western, the female. All the animals were divided into the animals of the day and those of the night. All the possessions of The People were divided into "soft goods and hard goods."

Here was an analogy to the Chinese opposites of Yin and Yang, of death and of life. I asked myself if different peoples in entirely different parts of the world thought and felt in the same way. I remembered the Lord of Duality of the Aztecs who was both good and evil, male and female.

THE NINTH NIGHT OF A NAVAJO CEREMONY

At the University Library in Berkeley I began to read the *Reports of the Bureau of Ethnology*. I read all the articles I could find on the Navajos but there was surprisingly little material available.

The reports written by Dr. Washington Matthews over the space of years from 1880 to his death in 1905 contained detailed descriptions of Navajo life and religion during a period when there were few or no observers on the reservation. His occasional note to the future student was so provocative I found myself interested in the man as well as in the results of his courageous and original research.

His translations of Navajo ritual make the treasure store from which many people have drawn inspiration and information. Some of them are scientific papers written for special occasions. Yet an Irish poet wrote them, and life and art and the spirit are in them.

Washington Matthews was born at Killeney, near Dublin, in 1843. After coming to this country with his father in 1847 he grew up and obtained his medical education in Dubuque, Iowa. He used his surgical knowledge in the Civil War, and later served as post doctor in various western forts. He was on the Navajo Reservation, at Fort Wingate, from 1880 to 1884 and from 1890 to 1894, traveling widely over it in the interim. He studied the Navajo language, became the friend of Navajo medicine men, saw many ceremonies, and recorded what he saw in books and magazine articles as well as in the government reports.

I made copies of the water color drawings he had made from the sand paintings of the Mountain and Night Chants. I enjoyed doing this so much I felt as though I were vaguely aware of the value of the symbols inherent in them. I began to make a collection of the copies of all the sand paintings I could find. Paradoxically enough, they were stimulating in the sense that modern art is, and yet they had a timeless quality.

These Navajo people whom we called "primitive" had religious rituals more developed than anything we knew of a similar nature. Indeed, no writer seemed to know the considerable number of their chant systems. It was said that there were over three hundred different sand paintings which were used in curing ceremonials.

My first experience of a major ceremony was on the ninth night of a Yeibechai. It is the ceremony which is easiest to see on the reservation.

The Night Chant is often called "Yeibechai" because there are so many yei, or gods, in its performances. The term is especially associated with Hastyéyalti, the maternal grandfather of the groups of Navajo divinities. He is the Talking God who comes to the aid of many of the heroes of the myths.

The Navajo yei are representatives of elemental forces, not gods in our use of the word. But we are compelled to call them so in translation. They are personified mysteries, supernatural beings who control great powers. They are "the far, mysterious ones." In their masks lies their essential holiness. There are sixteen gods and goddesses invoked in the rites of the Night Chant.

Dr. Matthews thinks the origin of some of these gods may have had something to do with the ancient cliff dwellers. Coming into the mountain and canyon country of northern Arizona and New Mexico, the Navajos may have projected some of their religious feelings on the men who lived in the strange and inaccessible cities of the cliffs—men who seemed to step off into the sky or walk on the faces of the high rocks. When they heard voices magnified by the deep canyon echoes they may have thought they heard the commands of a talking god.

The branch of the Night Chant usually given is known as "In the Rocks of the Canyon." It is one of four major versions of the chant.

Its setting and its "persons of the drama" are important. But most necessary to recognize and understand it is the traditional idea

behind the many acts and impersonations. To do so we must imagine we are in need of healing. For what reason or reasons we may
be as vague or as definite as the Navajo patient.

The ceremony is given primarily for the curing of a patient or
patients. But the chant systems include initiation rites for other
members of the tribe as well as general blessing for all those present. They are also the occasion for the religious and social gather-
ings of The People.

The patient may be wasting away with a disease or he may have
had a series of bad dreams. He may have overindulged in a favor-
ite pastime such as gambling or hunting, and so need to be brought
back to the "right way" where everything is done in due proportion.
He may be feeling tired all over and think that someone has stolen
his life energy. So the effects of witchcraft may have to be exor-
cised. Whatever the constellating circumstance, the Navajo does
not resort to physical diagnosis for a classification of his illnesses.

The People know that a psychic illness is as real as a physical
one. The outer manifestation of disease only indicates the real
cause, the lack of harmony between the great natural powers and
the earth men. The "one to be sung over" is out of the perfect
rhythm which exists between the yei and the little earth people.
For disease is discordant life. And health is the natural evidence
of the "way of beauty" between the gods and men.

This state of well-being is translated as fitness, or accord, or
beauty, but it means much more than these in the Navajo language.
It connotes a state of health which is both physical and spiritual—
"beauty within" as well as "beauty without." It implies a condition
of rapport with the gods, and with it goes a feeling of great peacefulness.

When the spirit is quiet and the inner body has become cool
again, that is a sign that the desired condition has been attained. For
unrest and fever imply the presence of evil. If the human-divine
rhythm has been broken, something must be done to re-establish it.
There must be a religious celebration.

As soon as the snakes are asleep and the frost is on the under
side of the herbs and shrubs which are to be gathered for medicine,
the Navajos say the "big sings" may begin. In October and No-
vember the harvests are in, and everyone has some leisure. It is

time for visiting and wearing one's best clothes. It is time to help some member of the clan who is giving a ceremony, to pray for rain and good crops, for "abundant hard goods and soft goods."

On a day long planned and eagerly awaited I found myself on the way. As we drove along from Oraibi in the late afternoon we were in the midst of a converging throng of The People. There were four of us in Lorenzo's car—Laura Armer, Lorenzo, a Navajo schoolgirl who was going to cook and keep our campfire going, and myself. I was "racing my eyes," as the Zuñi raven says, on a spectacle so dramatic that my senses could hardly accept it. There was color everywhere—moving, quickening color, and the most beautiful silver and turquoise jewelry.

The costumes of the women were remarkable for the vivid contrasts of blouses and skirts. The long, full sateen skirts were orange or bright green or black. On the wide flounces were many rows of rickrack braid of varied shades. The plush or velveteen blouses with high collars and long sleeves were red or bright blue or cinnamon color. On the collars and up and down the sleeves were many silver buttons. And there were great necklaces of silver and turquoise, many bracelets, earrings and rings studded with turquoise—turquoise everywhere. It was the perfect color against the brown of the skin tones.

They carried their family wealth in their turquoise and silver. But some massive strings of white shell, coral, and turquoise beads were especially attractive, for one seemed to realize that these were the older forms of adornment.

The men were dressed as gaily as the women, if not more so. They wore big, silver concha belts. Their brilliantly colored satin and velveteen shirts were very becoming to the dark, reserved faces. Many of them sported new "ten gallon" Stetson hats with silver bands around the crowns, but there were also many silk handkerchiefs tied around the heads and some badger-skin caps.

The Mongolian slant of the eyes was accented by the straight black hair and prominent cheekbones. Both the men and women had heavy, long, black hair. It was caught up in big double knots and tied with white string at the base of the neck. Only the boys who had been away to school had short hair.

The high, henna-colored buckskin moccasins with their share

of silver buttons seemed the perfect footwear for the desert earth, and they looked very comfortable.

If you can imagine these brightly dressed, handsome people on horseback, you will glimpse a part of the animation of the scene. Some of the fathers and mothers had children before and behind them on the saddles. Older members of the families sat on the floors of the farm wagons surrounded by cooking utensils and haunches of mutton. Young mothers sat with their babies held carefully on their cradle-boards.

The women of The People, by the way, are very influential and make many of the tribal arrangements. The children belong to the clans of their mothers. The women own the sheep and weave the very marketable Navajo rugs. They therefore control a large share of the tribal income. They have the right to divorce a man if he is not what they consider a good husband. When marriages take place the man goes to live near the clan of his wife.

Important matters are decided by the older women in consultation with their clan brothers and uncles. Amusingly enough, they often arrange a kind of agreeable polygamy. If the woman of the hogan has too much work to do, too many sheep to tend, she will invite a younger sister or niece to live with her and be a second wife to her husband. She accepts any children of the marriage as her own children. Consequently the Navajo often refers to "my mothers" instead of to a single female relative. And, of course, all of his maternal aunts are his "mothers," too.

As I sat watching the women around me I realized there were few or no unmarried women among The People. Yet I knew the government and the missionaries were trying to change these domestic relations. And I wondered what price spinsterhood!

We were all verging toward a spot called Where the Rocks Stand Out by the Cottonwood Trees, a piece of virgin earth in a little valley. It had been chosen as appropriate because no ceremony had ever been given there and no one had ever lived just there. Contrary to our belief that spiritual grace is only to be found in the church or consecrated ground where all religious ceremonies must be held, The People believe that only a place which has been unpolluted by human use can be the effective base of a curing rite. The place where the medicine hogan is built is also chosen because it is near a water supply and because wood may be procured for the fires at night.

As we went down the little incline toward the brush shelter of the family who were giving the chant we saw hundreds of Navajos making ready little camps, hobbling the horses near stacks of alfalfa, getting wood for their cooking fires. Everyone was very busy. Even the little children were gathering chips or taking care of smaller brothers and sisters.

Lorenzo said there were over a thousand of them, and more were coming in from all directions. Yet everything was quiet, peaceful and orderly, and an air of great purposefulness seemed to pervade the little valley.

As the evening light changed we made a camp to one side of the clearing. Ava, our Navajo schoolgirl, quickly spread a large tablecloth and placed much good food on it. A small cooking fire of aromatic pinyon nearby held the ever-present coffee-pot, and on a grill sputtered the sides of mutton which are so succulent a part of every Navajo feast. Lorenzo chuckled delightedly as we ate the ribs like ears of corn, without benefit of knives and forks. There was fresh peach jam on little rolls of bread fried in mutton fat, and very sweet corn of all colors on little ears. There were musk melons and watermelons and big tin cups of fragrant coffee.

The obvious social aspects of the gathering around us were amusing to watch. Marriageable sons and daughters were being subtly exhibited in all their velveteen finery, highlighted by the family jewels. The "noble, white metal" of the beads and bracelets shone in the light of the fires. Everyone had come not only to participate in the prayers and to hear the songs, but to gossip, to gamble, to race horses, to feast and to otherwise have a happy time.

The medicine hogan, a large circular structure of logs and adobe, was at the left of a sizable cleared space. Its single doorway was open to the east because that was the direction of the dawn and of least evil. Between it and the greenroom was the dancing floor, the stage for the outer drama of the ninth night. The greenroom, or dressing room of the god-actors, was a big corral made of evergreen boughs.

The twelve ceremonial fires were lighted, six on either side of the dancing floor. These fires represented the two canyon banks of the scene of the myth.

And then we heard the call of the Talking God, "Whu-hu-hu-hu," four times, coming louder and louder. In the silence, stirred only by the crackling of the fires, you could distinguish the shuffling of moccasined feet, and the shaking of rattles. Such significant sound! It was beginning rhythm, tentative, slow, then gradually increasing in volume.

The Chanter and a middle-aged Navajo woman patient came out of the medicine hogan and stood just outside the doorway. The woman held a basket filled with corn meal. From the near darkness toward them came the masked figures of the Talking God and the four Atsálei, the first four dancers. These men represented the four directions of the world as well as the Chiefs of the Corn, Rain, Plants and Pollen. They moved slowly up to the patient to be sprinkled with the holy corn meal. It was her sacrificial offering to them.

A long prayer followed, like part of a communion service. It was the most memorable moment of the whole night. In a low, chanting voice the medicine man would say a line, then pause as the woman repeated it. The dancers were swaying back and forth to its quiet stresses, lifting their feet slowly at appointed pauses in the prayer. A male divinity, a thunderbird god, was being invoked. He was supposed to live with the other gods at Tségihi, the place mentioned in the beginning.

The prayer was an invocation of the rain powers. The symbols on the masks and in the details of the costumes had to do with clouds, with the falling of water, with growing things.

> In Tségihi,
> In the canyon of the dawn,
> In the house of the twilight,
> In the house of the dark cloud,
> In the house of the male rain,
> In the house of the female rain,
> In the house of the pollen,
> Where the dark cloud curtains the doorway,
> The path to which is on the rainbow,
> Where the lightning serpent stands above,

O, male divinity,
With your moccasins of dark cloud,
Come to us.
With your leggings of dark cloud,
Come to us.
With your shirt of dark cloud,
Come to us.
With your headdress of dark cloud,
Come to us.

With the dark thunder above you,
Come to us, soaring.
With the dark rain-cloud below you,
Come to us, soaring.
With the far darkness of the dark cloud,
Come to us, soaring.
With the far darkness of the male rain,
Come to us, soaring.
With the far darkness of the dark mist,
Come to us, soaring.

With the far darkness of the female rain,
Come to us, soaring.
With the lightning serpent high above,
Come to us, soaring.
With the rainbow high over your head,
Come to us, soaring.
With the darkness on the ends of your wings,
Come to us, soaring.
With the darkness on the earth,
Come to us.

With these let the foam float on the water
Over the roots of the great corn plant.
I have made a sacrifice for you.
I have prepared the tobacco for you.

My feet restore for me.
My body restore for me.
My mind restore for me.
My voice restore for me.

Today take away the evil from me.
Far away you have taken it.
And happily I recover.
Happily my legs regain their power.
Happily my inner body becomes cool.
Happily my eyes regain their power.
Happily my head becomes cool.
Happily I hear again.
Happily I walk.
Feeling light within me, I walk.

Now abundant dark clouds I desire.
Abundant dark mists I desire.
Abundant passing showers I desire.
Abundant plants and pollen I desire.
Happily may fair white corn
To the ends of the earth
Come with you.
Happily may fair blue corn
To the ends of the earth
Come with you.
Happily may fair yellow corn
To the ends of the earth
Come with you.

Happily may fair corn of all colors
To the ends of the earth
Come with you.
Happily may fair plants of all kinds
To the ends of the earth
Come with you.
Happily may fair jewels of all kinds
To the ends of the earth
Come with you.

In beauty the old men will regard you.
In beauty the old women will regard you.
In beauty the young men will regard you.
In beauty the young women will regard you.
In beauty the boys will regard you.
In beauty the girls will regard you.

In beauty the children will regard you.
Happily as they all go to their homes
They will regard you.
May their roads home
Be on the peaceful trail.

In beauty, I walk.
With beauty before me, I walk.
With beauty behind me, I walk.
With beauty above me, I walk.
With beauty below me, I walk.
With beauty all around me, I walk.
With beauty within me, I walk.
It is finished in beauty.
It is finished in beauty.
It is finished in beauty.
It is finished in beauty.

Then the real dancing began. Lasting with short intervals of silence through the night, it ended as the first light of dawn showed in the eastern sky.

Different troupes of dancers and singers performed at given times before the medicine hogan. In the Náakai Dance six gods and six goddesses were led onto the scene by Hastyéyalti and followed by Tonénili, the Water Bearer, who played the part of a clown. This dance was repeated at forty-minute intervals throughout the eight or nine hours of darkness.

For many weeks in widely scattered communities men had been practicing for this performance. Each group therefore tried to do it more perfectly than any other. The parts of the Yébaad, or goddesses, were also played by the men. Shaking rattles, weaving in and out in the established manner, they bent and sang and gestured. The dance seemed to follow a circular pattern. Touching the earth with their rattles, they made the sound of the rain. They reached to heaven with their outstretched arms, persuading the celestial water to fall. Then they bent to pull the nourishing corn plants up. Over and over, they were helping it all to happen. Then the voices would trail off; there would be a silence and the dancers would troop back to the greenroom to remove the masks.

The audience was appreciating each performance, comparing the men from Pinyon to the men from around Black Mountain. The feasting was going on all the time. People were moving from one campfire to another, shaking hands, saying little.

In the medicine hogan, to which the Chanter and the patient had withdrawn, many songs and prayers were being sung. We were told that two hundred and fifty-two songs in a specified sequence were chanted there on the ninth night. And seventy-two other songs preceded the singing of this night.

As the first light began to come, the medicine man and the patient came out of the hogan and stood facing the east. Everyone in the gathering stood up and faced the east. Sleepy babies were picked up and held facing the growing light. Everyone was silently praying to the dawn, that its purity and strength might enter into them. Everyone was "breathing in the dawn." At that moment the bluebird song was sung.

> He has a voice.
> He has a beautiful voice.
> The bluebird has a voice
> That flows in gladness.
> Just at daybreak he calls.
> The bluebird calls.

It was the benediction.

The People were gathering themselves together to begin the blessed way home. All the household goods were being placed on the wagons. The men were saddling the horses. The mood of peaceful reverence was giving way to the busy scene of departure. Silent farewells were being said. One old woman near me took the hand of another old woman and just held it, looking into the eyes of her friend. Then each went to the family wagon to help in the packing. Soon all the trails were filled with happy, departing people. Some of the men were singing.

Laura and Lorenzo had been willing to bet that I would not be able to stay awake during the whole performance, that I would go to sleep in the car part of the time. But I had been so absorbed in watching the various dance groups and in going from fire to fire with my coffee cup that I was surprised when the peculiar grey light began to come. I was comprehending a little what it meant to a people to have living symbols.

Dr. Matthews spent twenty-one years collecting the material for his volume on the Night Chant. He wrote that he could have filled two more large volumes if he had been able to gather all the lore pertaining to it.

CHANTS, MYTHS AND GODS

Within the last twenty-five years a member of the Navajo tribe in need of a curative ceremony might have chosen among many chant systems. The choice seems to be growing smaller and smaller as the years pass. Today an interested observer might follow the patient through a Shooting Chant, a Night Chant or a Mountain Chant, among the major rites.

In a secondary group of possibilities there would be the Wind Chant, the Feather Chant, the Big Star Chant, the Eagle Chant and the Red Ant Chant. The Bead Chant is very rarely given now because it takes a large number of valuable properties.

If you were lucky you might see a Hail Chant, a Water Chant, a Coyote Chant, the Chant of Waning Endurance, or the Hozóni, the Chant of Beauty. The male half of this Chant of Beauty is called the Chant of Heavenly Beauty; the female half, the Chant of Earthly Beauty.

Of course, the so-called Squaw Dance, which was originally a war ceremony, may often be seen. And the short and adaptable Blessing Way may be sung over hotel or hogan, Anglo or Navajo, as the occasion proves auspicious at any time of the year.

Other chantways mentioned by investigators include a Rain Chant, a Deer Chant, a Knife Chant, a Vein Chant, a Dog Chant, a Raven Chant, a Wound Chant, an Arrow Chant and an Awl or Needle Chant. We also hear of many witchcraft ceremonies, some of which are described as "reversed chants." Generally speaking, each chant has a male branch and a female branch, each of these in turn having an "according to holiness" and an "according to evil" way of presentation.

We know today that many of the older ceremonies have been forgotten, and we have also the evidence of a trend to combine former separate systems. The latest chantway which I have seen on the reservation was the male branch of a Shooting Chant given Mountain Chant Way with a fire dance. This was the "according to holiness" aspect of the rite since parts of the Blessing Way were included and the use of the sun-house screen was an important detail of the last days.

So one has to study as many chant systems as possible in order to guess at their former outlines. For purposes of scientific study this is very difficult. But it makes a fascinating "pattern assemblage" for the student of literature and the ethnopsychologist.

The myth is the skeletal framework of the Navajo ritual practices. It is a long tale of a religious nature which "ties in" all the songs, prayers, sand paintings and other elements. The Navajo medicine man has to know his myths very thoroughly because each incident in its proper sequence reminds him of the act to be performed or the prayer to be sung.

There are possibly twenty or twenty-five major chantways. A number of them overlap each other in story content, varying in material as the chant is given in its blessing form or in its exorcistic aspect.

Behind all the myths and their variants seems to lie the Origin or Creation Myth. Most of the rite-myths belong to a special ceremony and are in the possession of the medicine man who performs that ceremony. But the Origin Myth seems to belong to the storytellers of the whole tribe. Its major themes are integrated into many of the other ceremonies.

Dr. Matthews, Dr. Goddard, Mr. A. M. Stephen, Father Berard Haile and Miss Wheelwright have published versions of it from different sources. But even with this body of differentiated material it is difficult to point out definite sequences. In fact, it is far easier to point out the many differences and contradictions in these accounts.

One is obliged to conclude that the great body of Navajo mythology is like "the great water" itself. It is an enormous and sometimes shapeless body now flowing to this shore, or climax of content, and now, with the tidal pull, returning to the depths of the abyss. Its source would seem to be the underground "lake of the soul," the "first water" in which all the forms are inherent.

The outlines which emerge from the water are like the first principles of an ancient world. They form by changing, by separating and coming together again. They are primordial thought forms of the human mind. Not only are they old—they are ever-living because they are born in the imagination of every man from early childhood irrespective of any influences coming from without. They are the archetypes, as St. Augustine called them.

We recognize many of these first elements from the fairy tales of our childhood. As the conception of the mythical characters develops, we become acquainted with the symbolic figures of the primitive view of the world. When the waters recede there is a dark and formless world inhabited by insects. Then animals and people appear. In the beginning animals *are* people and people *are* animals. The amorphous figures of the lower worlds become the prototypes of men and women in the upper worlds. Later they become gods and winds and stars and thunderbirds in a higher world of sky and clouds.

Gradually we become acquainted with the Hero and the Holy Twins, the Earth Mother and the Sky Father, the Witch Woman, the Wise Old Man, the Hermaphrodite, the Spiritual Guide, the Friendly Animals, the Shadow, the Guardians of the Doors, the Monsters, the Spirit of Evil and Mischief, and many other archetypal forms.

We go with the hero on his difficult journey. He must break the taboos of his people in order to become the medicine man. He begins as a beggar or poor wanderer on the face of the earth. He has often been disgraced and distrusted by everyone around him. But he is helped by the gods and given a friendly guide and spiritual comforter. He makes the descent into the underground world, secures the treasure of new knowledge, and makes the ascent into the light of the upper world. He teaches his wisdom to a younger brother in the form of a new ceremony or chant. Then he goes to live with the gods in another world of eternal knowledge.

The gods and goddesses of The People form a very interesting American pantheon. Some of them are in a family group. Others represent the spirits of the desert terrain. They carry the projections of the various ideas of spiritual and physical power which the Navajos have developed. They seem to be relative beings. Sometimes they are especially divine and at other times they are endearingly human.

There are a very large number of them. It is almost impossible to make an inclusive list of the Navajo hierarchy. Beside the holy family of Estsánatlehi, the Turquoise Goddess and Changing Woman, and the group of elder gods, or yei, there are many gods who belong to various localities. In fact each elder god may have his special manifestation in certain canyons and mountains. There are also the animal gods which are held in high esteem, especially the snakes and bears.

And then there are the enemy gods and Coyote. There would not be so many holy ones, old Seginnie told me, if there were not evil spirits and devils. So Coyote obligingly engenders evil, although he is known at first only as the scolder or mischief maker.

Mr. and Mrs. Coolidge have counted over three hundred birds, insects, animals and reptiles which are invoked as holy in the prayers. I have counted over a hundred personages in the chant drama. When we add to these twelve lightnings, twelve rains, fourteen winds, and so on, we can understand why The People had to have seven mountains instead of one Olympus to house their gods.

So we must remember they are the yei, these mysterious, supernatural beings. They are not in any sense moral beings who decide what is good and what is evil. It is simply stated that to be in harmony with their decisions is to be fit and well, to have well-being inside oneself as well as outside oneself, to "walk on the trail of beauty."

If we were to choose a "master symbol" for the Navajos as a people, it would have to be a perfect piece of turquoise. Though mined from the earth it is the brilliant, light blue color of the desert sky at noonday. And therefore in some way it represents a totality of sacred values. This choice would be understandable to anyone who knows The People and their part of the United States. Therefore it seems especially fitting that their most sacred god or goddess should be Estsánatlehi, the Turquoise Goddess and Changing Woman.

This most beneficent woman who becomes the mother of the

savior gods seems, at times, to have the characteristics of the oriental Kwan Yin, and at other times, the aspects of a Greek nature goddess. Her name means, literally, "the woman who rejuvenates or transforms herself." She grows from a baby to a beautiful young woman, becomes middle-aged and old, and then returns to the condition of a young girl again. She passes through an endless number of lives, changing as the seasons change, but never dying.

Her birth is supposed to be from a small turquoise image found upon a mountain top after Father Sky and Mother Earth have come together. There are numerous stories of her miraculous birth and discovery. In some of them she has a twin sister, Yolkáiestsan, the White Shell Woman.

Estsánatlehi becomes the wife of the Sun, or Sun Bearer, and the mother of Nayenezgáni, the young warrior god who is to slay the enemy monsters. Sometimes she is spoken of as the mother of both warrior gods, or holy twins. At other times the White Shell Woman is called the mother of the younger, Tobadsistsíni, the Child of the Water.

In one version of the Origin Myth, the Turquoise Woman makes the sun and the moon from her two breasts, the sun from turquoise beads hidden in her right breast, the moon from white shell beads in her left breast.

In the Bead Chant she is said to have five daughters. Four of them are born from various parts of her body, but the fifth daughter is born of her spirit. This last daughter becomes the mother of the hero of the chant, so we are justified in thinking of Changing Woman as the grandmother as well as the mother of heroes. She also gives birth to herself as her own daughter by rolling a piece of skin from under her left breast. She has created many of the Navajo clans also from the skin of her body. We can define her as the Earth Mother as well as the daughter of the Earth Mother. But it is only by association in the myths that we can at all outline her great and sacred proportions.

At one time in her metamorphosis she goes to the western home which has been prepared for her by her sun-husband. It is on an island off the coast of the western ocean. From there she sends the abundant rains of summer and the thawing breezes of spring. To her the Sun Bearer goes after the work of the day is done. Of course, he cannot go to her every night, The People say. When the days are dark and grey the Sun Bearer must stay with his other wife in her eastern home.

The Turquoise Goddess is so revered it is forbidden to make any representation of her. Her home is sometimes depicted in the center of a sand painting, but her actual presence would seem to be implied through the presence of her sons. In one version of the Hail Chant it is said that even the gods must not look on her. As twelve of them sit in the middle of the holy hogan they are told to bow their heads and not to look up as she enters and seats herself in the center.

Many of the other gods in the myths are changing persons, also. Her two sons become four sons as their attributes develop. Coyote changes from yellow to white as he steps back and forth on the twin trails of good and evil. The blue and black thunder gods change their roles according to necessity. There is even a character in the Feather Chant called Dinné-altsó-natlehi, or He-Who-Changes-Into-Everything.

Yet there is no inconsistency to the Navajo mind in all of these changing forms and figures. Professor Reichard discusses this fact very interestingly in her book on the sand paintings of the Shooting Chant. She thinks that it is only when we try to chart these forms in a white man's rational way that we run into difficulties.

The holy twins, or young warrior gods, would seem to be next in importance to the Turquoise Goddess. Whether they are referred to as her sons or as the sons of herself and her sister, they are always called young brother gods.

Nayenezgáni, whose name means Slayer of the Enemy Gods, is the elder of the two and always plays the leading role. Tobadsistsíni, his younger brother, sometimes called the Child of the Water, often disappears from the myth altogether. He is a kind of shadow brother to the hero of the story.

Nayenezgáni is connected with light as he walks upon the tops of the mountains. Tobadsistsíni is a god of valleys and foothills, of darkness and of moisture. One walks proudly, the other humbly.

After their miraculous births they grow to manhood in four days. Their chief mission is to kill the monsters who are destroying The People. They are also supposed to help warriors in battle and to assist people who have been made ill through witchcraft.

There would seem to be no father god in the Navajo conception of deity. The Sun or Sun Bearer is sometimes spoken of as omnipotent in the heavens, but it is assumed that he was made long after the birth of the first people. The Talking God, Hastyéyalti, in his capacity as maternal grandfather, comes close to this idea, but he is no Zeus with a powerful family of sons and daughters around him. He is, however, a kind of ancestor god who gives helpful advice and guides events to the divine solution. He has a companion who is known as Hastyéhogan, the Home God, or god of the Navajo hogan and farm. While the Talking God is the god of the east and of the dawn, the Home God is the god of the west and of the sunset.

All the yei are supposed to be married and to have families of their own. The male yei are called the Yébaka and the female yei, the Yébaad.

Among the other yei are Hastyésini, the Navajo God of Fire, Hastyéoltoi, the Goddess of Hunting, Hastyéeltsi, the God of Racing, and Hadastsísi, the Whipping God. The God of Fire is called the Black God and the God of Racing, the Red God.

A yellow-haired god known as Begóchiddi appears to live up in the sky and is referred to as the maker of domestic animals and of certain game. But reports of Begóchiddi are very contradictory. He is called the youngest son of the Sun, and his mother is described as a flower which the Sun made pregnant. He is a hermaphrodite and the first maker of pottery. He would seem to be somewhat like the Quetzalcoatl of the Mexicans, who is also spoken of as yellow-haired.

Tonénili, the Water Bearer of the Navajo gods, is a very interesting figure concerning whom we do not have enough information. Like the Roman Aquarius he preserves and cares for the water of the gods. In the Navajo meaning this is a special kind of water in a pair of blue and black jars. Brought from the four corners of the world and blessed by the gods, it has become a holy water which is especially effective against the monsters.

The Spider Woman is the underground guardian of special talismans, such as the magic breath-feather. She helps heroes to attain necessary knowledge in the underground world. There seems to be more than one of these spider guides.

Níltsi, the wind god, also has many aspects. He is spoken of as the son of Hastyéhogan in one of the myths. As the Spirit Wind he sits on the shoulder of the hero and whispers in his ear.

Tóntso, the messenger of the gods, is a kind of large fly called the harvest fly. He also guides the hero, and his wisdom is simple and homely.

The Great Snake, Klíshtso, appears in so many roles it is impossible to define him in a few phrases. He is identified with everything from a constellation to the corral, or dark circle of branches, used in the ninth night of the Mountain Chant.

What is important to remember as we see the holy ones in the various rites is that they can be represented by the medicine man. In turn and all at once, the Chanter can identify himself and later the patient with their mysterious qualities. He therefore assumes the power of the gods as he invokes them, and in his own being personifies all their changing forms.

NAVAJO SONGS

The songs of our southwestern Indians are their sustaining creative expression. Just as corn provides sustenance for their physical lives, so does singing provide spiritual food. This seems to be literally true in the singing of the ritual songs, for to these people song shows the trail of communication with the gods. A song from a ceremony is generally a prayer, and a prayer is certainly a song.

The Papago Indians of southern Arizona are very aware of the power which comes through singing. All through the year at their various fiestas they generate divine power by their songs.

"The songs are mounting," they say, as they approach the threshold of vision in their rituals. A spiritual idea, a reassurance through the grace of communication with the guardian animal spirit, expressed in the potent sound of a man's voice raised to the skies—is there not a cosmic secret revealed here? To give a rhythmic form to the intuitive knowledge—should not that be the height of a man's spiritual wisdom? To be again in harmony with the rhythm of the gods one must make harmonious syllables, for the form of the prayer is very important. By themselves the words are helpless, they say.

"I sing; therefore I am strong," says the enlightened Papago.

Juan Xavier is a friend of mine from the Papago Reservation near Tucson. During the Second World War he started to work in a near-by factory which was assembling parts of airplanes. He worked on the afternoon shift from three o'clock until twelve at night. All morning he worked on his farm. In the factory there was a great roar of noise about him which was very hard for the desert man to endure. He thought he would have to give up the job, although he wanted to help in the war effort. He said that the white man's engines were too strong for the peace of his spirit. One day, when he was on the point of deciding to quit, as he stared at a great wheel going around he heard a song come out of it. It was a song with a message for him, and he was hearing it in the midst of all the disturbance. He told his wife that night that everything was all right and he was going to keep right on working at the factory.

They say that the power of song is so great you can influence the gods through it. This is true especially if the song came to you in a dream or vision, for the gods probably sent it to you. It was like that in the beginning. All songs were ordered. They were gifts.

The power of song is so great that if another person hates you and is making a song against you, if you can begin to sing before he does, he is powerless to hurt you.

Or, if you have offended a god and are out of harmony with the supernatural ones, you can conciliate him by learning his special song. You can call him by his secret name in a song and cause him to wonder and forgive and re-create you. Every god and man and animal and bird has a secret name which is a sound or combination of sounds which stand for his being. If you know the sounds of the thunder and lightning powers, you can call upon them in your songs, and they will be compelled to come to your singing. For may not a song be of the very power of nature?

Something of the power of the poet through all the ages, of the spokesman of the meaning of things, is realized by the Navajo Indian as he sings—as he sings while he is preparing to hunt, as he walks around his farm as he plants his corn, as he gambles with his friends, as he rides along lonely mountain trails singing the songs of blessing for the journey. They sing as they build the hogans, as they light the fires, as they arise in the morning and as they go to sleep at night. There are songs for work of all kinds and songs for women in childbirth. There are even songs for the unborn child.

The songs which belong to the religious rituals have the authority of tradition behind them. They must be learned exactly, syllable for syllable. But the Navajos improvise songs, too. I have watched a group of Navajo men exchanging songs with a group of Taos men as they squatted on their heels and played with pebbles. They would take a phrase and develop it. One man sings it, as though he were saying, "Do you know this one?" Other men who know the song join in—then the voices of the other tribal chorus as they master it. It seems something like the experimentation with jazz phrases among Negro musicians.

A Navajo man is "giving," and his gift turns into a new song. If you make a song it can become a very special gift. A song may even be "your holy child." One Navajo man said to Dr. Hill, "I am very poor. I do not own one song."

While you are listening you realize the very vigorous rhythmic patterns which the songs have. There are sudden, sharp, accented beats which come often at the ends of words. The accompaniment is generally the shaking of the gourd rattle or the tapping on the inverted basket. (The Navajos do not use drums in the way the Pueblo Indians do.)

The effect of Navajo singing on the American listener is often monotonous. The tones of the voices are pitched very high and are often nasal in quality. Some records of them have been made by Laura Boulton for the Victor Company. Dr. Matthews collected many phonographic records which were later studied and commented on by Professor John Comfort Fillmore. He concludes that they throw much light on the problem of form spontaneously assumed by natural folk songs. He says that the most striking characteristic of the metrical grouping of tones is the freedom with which the singer changes from one elementary rhythm to another.

Natalie Curtis Burlin gives the words and music to a number of Navajo songs in her collection of songs called *The Indian's Book*. Dr. W. W. Hill of the University of New Mexico translates the material of many songs in his book, *The Agricultural and Hunting Methods of the Navajo Indians*. Miss Wheelwright has published some songs based on the Creation Myth in her book on this subject. In the Museum of Navajo Ceremonial Art at Santa Fe she has collected over fifteen hundred songs on records.

Mrs. Dane Coolidge in *The Rainmakers* emphasizes the fact that when the southwestern peoples sing they are weaving magic. She thinks that the songs of birds may be the prototypes of human song, since the birds are considered by these peoples to be divine messengers. The themes of the songs generally have to do with rain, with corn, with animals. One might add here, somewhat facetiously, that the theme song of the southwest might be addressed to an animal to ask him to bring the rain to make the corn grow.

Love songs are seldom sung. One such song to the beloved, Mrs. Coolidge reports, calls her "my little breath"—another way of saying "my little soul."

There would seem to be an innate Indian wisdom in the fact that it is considered dangerous to make songs about love. The Indian evidently knows something of the possible projection of the soul on the beloved object, and he also knows this is the age-old opportunity for witches. Why then tie up part of your soul forever in a song?

Herbert Spinden in his book on southwestern poetry says that a word accompanied by a musical sound is a potent symbol, as potent as a painted or sanded symbol. He thinks the main source of these songs is in dreaming. If you dream of a bear, for instance, the dream may mean that you now have too much of the power of the bear. You may have to have a ceremony said over you to cleanse you from so much power. In any event you must make a song about the dream to make its effect less powerful. He tells us that among the Plains Indians there were dream societies formed by men who had dreamed of the same animals or natural elements. The Ghost Dance Cult of 1850–80 which gave the United States government so much trouble was really a dream cult, producing certain ceremonial patterns as the result of dream experiences.

As will be seen in the translations of the songs which follow, poetic figures of speech abound. Dr. Matthews thinks that all the figures of speech which are known to our poets are known to Navajo song makers. He thinks that the most interesting songs are those connected with the religious rites. He stresses the fact that if there were only significant words to remember, the medicine man's task would be much easier. But the songs consist also of archaic vocables and meaningless sounds like the "fol-de-rol" of sailors' songs. Nor may any syllable ever be omitted or changed. Preludes and refrains of these syllables are characteristic parts of the songs. They are never alike in any two songs. The medicine man seems to remember them by means of these preludes just as we may remember a poem by recalling the first line. Of course, preludes and refrains may be partly meaningful, but they are never wholly so.

The reason that the medicine man can remember the songs lies in the myth. The songs are strung on the body of the story of the myth like the larger beads on the rosary string. It seems to me permissible to conclude that whenever the story of the myth wanders and is inconsequential it is probably the occasion for the introduction of a song sequence. There may be comparatively meaningless sentences in the myth devised as aid to the medicine man's memory. As the story of the myth advances and there is decided action, obvious changes in the music occur.

The American poet Eda Lou Walton, in her study of Navajo poetry, says that the Navajo is not ignorant of the value of rhyme in his songs. He produces this by the repetition of significant sounds or syllables without meaning rather than by selecting words with similar endings. She thinks the latter and more difficult form is also employed.

One of the most interesting of the song sequences is known as the Songs in the Garden of the Home God. These songs number forty in all. Sometimes they are sung as part of the Night Chant. Hastyéhogan, the Hogan or House God, also seems to have especial care of the cornfields. There is more than one of these divinities according to the locality. These songs concern the Home or Farm God of Broad Rock, in Canyon de Chelly, Arizona. I have included some of them in the story called "In the Garden of the Home God."

In the songs which follow I have used Dr. Matthews' work whenever I could. I am also grateful to Dr. Hill for permission to use some of his material. Certain translations have been shortened and condensed, and many preludes and choruses omitted. I have tried to keep the poetical imagery of the Navajos. The form has to be often an inadequate English one. But I understand that many Navajo words have figurative meanings, so I comfort myself with the thought that literal translations would not be necessarily representative. In fact a number of translations I have seen have entirely obscured the poetry of Navajo ideas. I feel that I am dealing here with artistic material, so that I am unable to be scientific at this point. The often deeply religious response of the Navajo to the beauty and meaning of Nature has to be interpreted by the artist as well as by the scientist, it seems to me. Certainly the Navajo categories are artistic and religious in nature rather than scientific, as Dr. Reichard has said. They are the irrational reactions of the poet and painter rather than the rational observations of the scientist.

Three Songs from the Night Chant

I

In the house of life I wander
On the pollen path,
With a god of cloud I wander
To a holy place.
With a god ahead I wander
And a god behind.
In the house of life I wander
On the pollen path.

2

Song of Dawn Boy

Where my kindred dwell
Near the red rock house
There I will wander.
I am the Dawn Boy,
Child of the White Corn.

On the trail of the pollen of dawn
I am wandering.
Where the dark rain cloud
Hangs low before the door
I am wandering.
In the house of long life
I will wander.
In the house of happiness
I will wander.
With beauty before me
I will wander.
With beauty behind me.
I will wander.
With beauty above me
I will wander.
With beauty below me
I will wander.
In old age traveling
On the trail of beauty
I will wander.
It shall be finished in beauty.

3
Song of the Dreamer to his Brother at the End of the Night Chant

"Farewell, my younger brother.
  The Gods have come for me.
  From the high, holy places
  The far, mysterious ones have come.
  You will never see me again.
  But when the showers pass over you
  And the thunders sound,
  You will say,
  'There is the voice of my elder brother.'
  And when the harvests ripen,
  And you hear the voices of birds,
  Of beautiful birds of all kinds,
  And the singing of grasshoppers,
  You will say,
  'There is the ordering of my elder brother.
  There is the trail of his mind.'"

Hunting Songs

1

Comes the deer to my singing,
Comes the deer to my song!
I am the black bird,
Beloved of the wild deer.
Comes the deer to my singing.
From the black mountain,
From the top of the mountain,
Down the trail coming,
Coming, coming now,
Comes the deer to my singing.
Through the flower pollen coming,
Coming, coming now,
Comes the deer to my singing.
Stamping, turning, coming,
Starting with his left front foot,
Coming, coming now,
Comes the deer to my singing.
Down the mountainside,
Coming, coming now,
Comes the deer to my singing.
Quarry of mine,
I am lucky in my hunting.
Comes the deer to my singing.
Comes the deer to my song.

2

He is making a home for me
Where there was no home.
He who is master of the male deer
Is making a home for me.
With dark pinyon boughs
He is making it.
He is making a home for me
Where there was no home.

He is making a home for me
Where there was no home.
He who is master of the female deer
Is making a home for me.

With blue pinyon boughs
He is making it.
He is making a home for me
Where there was no home.

He is building a fire for me
Where there was no fire.
The Black God is building a fire.
With dark stones
He is building it.
He is building a fire for me
Where there was no fire.

He has given me the fire,
He has given me fuel.
The Rat Man and Woman
Have brought me the fuel.
He has given me water
From the Otter Man.
He has made a home for me
Where there was no home.

They are thinking about it.
They are thinking about my hunting.
The Talking God and the Black God,
The female one who knows the game,
My home shall be full of game.
In death the game obey me.

If any held evil toward me
It shall not come to pass
Because you will protect me.
With your dark horn
You will protect me.
I shall have great luck with game.
I shall have good luck with male game,
I shall have good luck with female game.
From the four directions
They shall stream to me.
At the doorway of the house
They will stand sideways to me.
I shall not miss their hearts.
In death they shall obey me.

3

Hunting Prayer to the Crow

You who travel by means of the black wind
Help me to the same power.
You who travel by means of the blue wind
Help me to the same power.
You who travel by means of the yellow wind
Help me to the same power.
You who travel by means of the white wind
Help me to the same power,
That I may do my hunting as you do,
That all evil will be dissolved from me,
Help me to your power.

Songs from the Mountain Chant

I

In the Place of the Emergence,
In the place where they came up,
In the holy mountains,
In the place where the people
Came up from the lower world to this world,
There were four mountains coming up.
Lo, in the north a black mountain standing,
In the east, a white mountain standing,
In the south, a blue mountain standing,
In the west, a yellow mountain standing.
And a god is standing on each mountain top.
Over the northern mountain I can see
The tail of my black bird floating.
It is my sacrifice, my treasure.
Over the eastern mountain I can see
The tail of the magpie floating.
It is my sacrifice, my treasure.
Over the southern mountain I can see
The tail of the hen-hawk floating.
It is my sacrifice, my treasure.
Over the western mountain I can see
The tail of the yellow bird floating.
It is my sacrifice, my treasure.

2

He stands on high, the holy young man,
On the rock where the black sheep called to him,
He stands on high with his great arrow,
His feathered arrow, his own sacred arrow,
Truly his own sacrifice and treasure.

She stands on high, the holy young woman,
On the rock where the black sheep called to her,
She stands on high with her great arrow,
Her feathered arrow, her own sacred arrow,
Truly her own sacrifice and treasure.

3

In a circle of sunbeam, his own sacred sign,
The holy young man is standing.
Truly with his treasure which makes him holy,
He is standing with his great arrow.
He is standing in a circle of sunbeams.

In a circle of rainbow, her own sacred sign,
The holy young woman is standing.
Truly with her treasure which makes her holy,
She is standing with her great arrow.
She is standing in a circle of rainbow.

4

The holy young man saw the mountain sheep,
Across two valleys and far beyond
He appeared with his slender horns
Standing on a high rock with his beautiful horns.

5

At the foot of the black mountain,
There in the circle of mountains,
The holy young man laid down his child.
At the foot of the blue mountain,
There in the circle of mountains,
The holy young woman laid down her child.

There were two gods on each mountain top,
And they said as they watched,
'Who learns our songs shall be our child.
Ahaláni!''

6

O, there lie the black mountains to the north,
And there lie my black cherry-sticks.
There lie my sacrifices, my treasures—
Go to get them!

O, there lie the blue mountains to the south,
And there lie my blue cherry-sticks,
There lie my sacrifices, my treasures—
Go to get them!

7

There was a maiden who became a bear,
And she walked and wandered far.
Far around her spread the land,
But it was not far to her.
Dim in the distance spread the land,
But it was not dim to her.

8

The young woman who became a bear
Set fire to the mountains.
As she journeyed on and on
There was a line of burning mountains.

The young man who became an otter
Set fire to the waters,
As he journeyed on and on
There was a line of burning waters.

9

The maiden who became a bear
Sought the gods and found them.
On the high mountain peaks
She sought the gods and found them.
Truly with her sacrifice, her treasure,
She sought the gods and found them.
Somebody doubts it, so I have heard.

The holy young woman sought the gods,
She sought the gods and found them.
On the summits of the clouds
She sought the gods and found them.
Truly with her sacrifice, her treasure,
She sought the gods and found them.
Somebody doubts it, so I have heard.

10

The darkness is passing.
The curtain of the dawn is hanging
Over the land of day.
For Dawn Boy it is hanging,
Like a great wreath it is hanging
Over the land of day.
For the Dawn God it is hanging.
From the place of daybreak
Before him it is hanging.
Behind him it is hanging.
In beauty it is hanging.
The curtain of dawn obeys his voice.

The darkness is passing.
The curtain of the dawn is hanging
Over the land of day.
For Daylight Girl it is hanging,
Like a great wreath it is hanging
From the land of yellow light.
For the Dawn Girl it is hanging.
Before her it is hanging.
Behind her it is hanging.
In beauty it is hanging.
The curtain of dawn obeys her voice.

11

Song of the Prophet to the River

Aháláni!
Greeting to my country
For which I am longing.

And greeting to the river
For which I am longing.
That flowing water, that flowing water—
My mind wanders toward it.
That broad water, that flowing water—
My mind wanders across it.
That old age river, that old age river—
My mind wanders across it.

12

In the place where the sun rises,
The holy young man has swallowed the arrow
And withdrawn it, slowly, slowly.
He has swallowed the great feathered arrow
And withdrawn it slowly.
The sun is satisfied.

In the place where the sun sets,
The holy young woman has swallowed the arrow,
And withdrawn it, slowly, slowly.
She has swallowed the arrow of cliff-rose
And withdrawn it slowly.
The moon is satisfied.

13

Prayer to the Prophet

Dsílyi Neyáni!
Reared in the mountains!
Lord of the mountains!
Chieftain!
I have made a sacrifice for you.
I have prepared the smoke for you.
My feet restore thou for me.
My legs restore thou for me.
My body restore thou for me.
My mind restore thou for me.
My voice restore thou for me.
Restore all for me in beauty and peace.
Make beautiful all that is before me.
Make beautiful all that is behind me.

Make beautiful all that is around me.
Make beautiful my words.
It is finished in beauty.
It is finished in beauty.
It is finished in beauty.
It is finished in beauty.

14

Song of the Prophet to his Deerskin Mask

When I called on you at any time
You always helped me, my pet.
You were alive once, my pet.
Take care of my life now.
Watch over me.

Gambling Songs from the Ketsicke Game

1

Wildcat Song

Is the foot of the wildcat sore, oh sore?
Are his feet so very sore?
He walks as though he were in pain.
He walks as though his old feet hurt him.

Yes, it is the old wildcat.
Truly it looks like the old wildcat.
His thighs are striped, I can see.
Yes, it is the old wildcat.

He was walking and he was walking.
He began to run down the hill at me.
But I ran right toward him
While he growled, he growled at me.

2

Bear Song

Whence comes he, the bear?
With those four, those four,
Those four, those four old shaggy legs?
Lo, he comes here on his four old shaggy legs.

3
Badger Song

The badger is always lying down,
Badger always lying down.
"Waurr," he says, lying down.
With that white streak down his forehead
Always lying down!

4
Little Owl Song

Shall I see the little burrowing owl?
Do I hope to find him down there?
Yes! Look at his crest stick up!
There he is, the little one!
The little burrowing owl!

5
Dove Song

Lo, the dove is flying.
The mourning dove is flying.
Toward the wide, white desert plain
See, the dove is flying.

Coo-coo, he picks them up.
Coo-coo, he picks them up.
Old glossy-breast picks them up.
Coo-coo, he picks them up.
With his shining head he picks them up.

Corn Planting Song

In the middle of the wide field
The corn has started to grow.
In both directions it is growing,
With roots growing down
And stalks growing up
In the middle of the wide field.
Now one is green.

Now two are green,
Now three and four.
And all is green
In the middle of the wide field.
For White Corn Boy and Yellow Corn Girl
Have come with their jewels
To make the corn green.

My good and everlasting corn,
It is arising.
The corn is growing
In the middle of the wide field.
My corn plants touch each other
In the middle of the wide field.
My corn makes a dark shadow
In the middle of the wide field.

Song of the Horse

My feet are made of mirage,
My bridle of strings of the sun.
My mane is like the white lightning.
My tail is like long black rain.
My eyes are big, spreading stars.
My teeth are of the white shell.
My belly is white as dawnlight.
My heart is of everlasting garnet.

Song of the Young War God

I have gone to the end of the earth.
I have gone to the end of the waters.
I have gone to the end of the sky.
I have gone to the end of the mountains.
I have found no one who was not my friend.

In a version of the Night Chant called the Crippled Twins Branch, there is a song which seems to me one of the most significant of the Navajo songs. I include it at this point. It is necessary to keep it in its context, however, so part of the myth must go with it.

The twin sons of a Navajo virgin and Talking God go on a journey to the land of the gods in order to be cured of their ills. One of them has lost his sight, the other has had his legs paralyzed. The blind boy carries his crippled brother on his shoulders to guide them. They know that they suffer because they have transgressed against the command of the gods. When they arrive at the home of the gods their first requests have been denied.

> They walked in silence down the canyon,
> And they mourned for what they had done.
> They knew not which way to go
> Or what new trail they should take.
> They wept as they walked along,
> And as they wept they began to sing.
> At first they made only sounds,
> But then there came singing words.
>
> They cried to their music
> And they turned their thoughts to song.
> The Holy Ones beyond them heard.
> They said to one another, wondering,
> "What are they saying in their song?"
> They sent the father to find out.
>
> Talking God overtook them and said,
> "The Holy Ones say you are to return.
> They wish to know about your song."
> The blind boy said, "We will not go.
> They told us to be gone in anger."
> But the crippled one said, "Let us return.
> Let us find out what they wish to say."
>
> The Holy Ones questioned them, and said,
> "What were you singing as you went along?"
> "We were not singing. We were crying,"
> Said the blind boy and his brother.
>
> "Why were you crying?" asked the gods.
> "We did not know what we were to do,"
> Said the crippled one and his brother.

"What kind of song was that you sang?"
Asked the grandfather of the gods.
"We surely heard the words of a song."
"We were not singing. We were crying."
They answered just the same.

But the fourth time of the asking
The crippled one began to reply,
"We were crying and crying,
But our crying turned into a song.
We never knew the song before.
My blind brother sang it first,
And this is what we sang:

'From the white plain where stands the water,
From there we come.
Bereft of eyes, one bears the other,
From there we come.
Bereft of limbs, one guides the other,
From there we come.

Where healing herbs grow by the waters,
From there we come.
With these our eyes we will recover,
From there we come.
With these our limbs we will recover,
From there we come.

From meadows green where ponds are scattered,
From there we come.
Bereft of eyes, one bears the other,
From there we come.
Bereft of limbs, one guides the other,
From there we come.

By springs where healing plants are growing,
From there we come.
With these our eyes we will recover,
From there we come.
With these our limbs we will recover,
From there we come.' "

The following lines show the Atsálei Song (from the beginning
of the ninth night of the Night Chant) as it looks in Dr. Matthews'

Óhohohó éhehehé héya yéya.
Óhohohó éhehehé héya yéya.
Hówani hówowówowów owé.
Hówani hówowówowów owé.
Hówani hóa hówani hó.
Hówani hóa héya heáhi oowé
Héya heáhi oohí.
Óhohohó héya heáhi ehéyeyíyayéa.
Oahóa hóa hówoa.
Éyehéyehéye óhoahó.
Éyehéyehéye óhoahó.
Éyehéyehéye.
Hábi niye hábi níye.
Hahozánaha, sihiwánaha
[The corn grows up, the rain comes down.]
Tsinatáa bílniya.
[The corn plant with it arrives.]
Aiáheóo aiáheó.
Sihiwánaha, hahozánaha.
[The rain comes down, the corn grows up.]
Tóbiazi bílniya.
[The child-rain with it arrives.]
Aiáheóo aiáheó.
Óhohohó éhehehé héya héya.

THE MEDICINE MAN

A comparative study of the medicine men of various American
Indian tribes would give us a composite picture of a strong and
developed human being. Beside the account of personal power
these men have left a record of service to their peoples. They have
been the old wise men, the doctors with knowledge of curative herbs
and the high priests of the religious ceremonies.

A partial list of some of their titles is revealing: Men of the
Dawn, Dreamers of the Gods, Summoners of the Spirit, The Lis-

teners, Revealers of Hidden Things, Those Possessed of Divine Fire, Keepers of the Faith, Priests of the Holy Way.

The Navajo medicine man is called the Hatáli, or Chanter. He is the supreme individual of the tribe. He is the conscious human being who tries to bring evil under ritual control. He is the Enlightener, for it is through him that a meaning is imparted to the life of The People.

Although there are many significant personalities among the Navajos, most of them live in an identity with the family and with the clan and its laws. This has been of necessity so, for much communal effort has been required for the purpose of survival in a barren country.

Therefore supreme individuals are needed to be the containers of the tribal values. These are spiritual values, of course, and it is the person who has developed himself through severe spiritual discipline who becomes the powerful medicine man or woman.

In the terms of modern analytical psychology the medicine man is an introverted intuitive type. Reaching into his inner depths in concentrated periods of introversion he has discovered the forms of the collective images. Today we know that the dominating ideas of the unconscious mind are peculiarly accessible to this type of human being.

In the history of his long service the medicine man has formulated his esoteric teaching in a body of sacred ceremonies equaled by few peoples of the world. He has given the unspoken thoughts and feelings of the men of his world a voice which speaks with authority. To all the contents of their deeply unconscious minds he has given a traditional form, a beautiful form. He has modified the universal images, making them peculiarly effective for his own race. Out of the depths of formless, chaotic fears he has made a noble religion and system of ethics. He has dispossessed the monsters. He brings the assurance that only the unknown thing is the evil thing. He says that what we really know we can bring under control in human consciousness.

His prayers are not petitions. They are statements of desired effects. The powers of the supernatural ones are described as present and operative in association with the needs of himself or his patient.

An example of the prayer of a Navajo medicine man is included here. I have condensed it from a version recorded by Dr. Matthews. It is really, as he says, a narrative poem. We do not know enough yet about the Navajo chants to place it in its mythological context, but it might be a part of the Hotchónji. Or it could belong to the exorcistic aspect of a number of the chants, if, as some investigators think, the material of the myths can be interchangeable according to the necessity recognized by the medicine man. Or this prayer might be part of a Coyote Chant, since most of the branches of this chant seem to have something to do with the exorcism of evil caused by witchcraft.

The medicine man who gave the prayer to Dr. Matthews was over seventy years of age. He said he had learned it in his youth from another very old man. He said it was the most potent prayer that he knew. It was so sacred it must not be repeated twice on the same day. It must be said through without stopping. No portion of it could ever be said by itself. It must be preceded by the sacrifice of tobacco in the making of prayer-sticks.

The medicine man had been telling the Creation Myth to Dr. Matthews, and he had become very uneasy. He said it was dangerous to have his mind wandering in the realms of the dead, that he might become diseased as a result. In telling the incidents which happened in the first four worlds, he felt that he might encounter evil effects if he did not placate the spirits met on his journey in the realms of the ancestors. He prayed sitting on the floor with his hands resting on his knees, his eyes open and fixed before him.

> From the high summits of the sacred mountains
> The Young Warrior Gods come for my sake.
> From the top of the black mountains
> Nayenezgáni comes for my sake.
> Over the white ridges of the foothills
> Tobadsistsíni comes for my sake.
> In the center they meet.
> Near the Place of the Emergence
> They meet for my sake.
>
> Although the smooth winds guard the door
> The Slayer of Enemy Gods opens the way.

He waves his long black wand for me.
Child of the Water, his younger brother,
Waves his blue wand to open the way.
For my sake they arrive together.
Through the first room of the black cloud
A way is opened for me.
Through the second room of the blue cloud
A way is opened for me.
Through the third room of the yellow cloud
A way is opened for me.
Through the fourth room of the white cloud
A way is opened for me.
Where the two red rivers meet and cross
A way is opened for me.

Through the first room of the black mountain
Although the Red Bear guards the door,
A way is opened for me.
Through the second room of the blue mountain
Although the Red Snake guards the door,
A way is opened for me.
Through the third room of the yellow mountain
Although the Red Coyote guards the door,
A way is opened for me.
Through the fourth room of the white mountain
Although the Red Hawk guards the door,
A way is opened for me.

In the entry of the red-floored house,
The House of the Woman Chieftain
In the center of the world,
Nayenezgáni opens a way for me.
Tobadsistsíni opens a way for me.
For my sake they arrive together.
In the doorway of her house,
By the fireplace of the house,
In the middle of the house,
In the back of the house,
A way is opened for me,
Where my feet are lying,
Where my legs are lying,

Where my body is lying,
Where my mind is lying,
Where the dust lies on my feet,
Where my spittle lies on the ground,
Where my hair lies on the ground,
Nayenezgáni puts his great stone knife
And his talking prayer-stick.
He puts them in my hand and with them
He turns me around as the sun goes.
So, I face him. And he says,
"Woman Chieftain, restore my grandson,
So, my grandson is restored to me.
Speak not to him or try to find him.
Now we start back with him.
Out of your house he is walking,
And I am behind him walking,
And my brother is behind me walking,
And we all go out together."

Through all the mountain rooms
They are returning with me.
Through the black clouds and the mists
They are returning with me.
We are climbing up together
To the Place of the Emergence.
Although the smooth winds guard the door,
We go out, returning home on this earth.
At the place where the coyotes race,
At the place where great gourds hang,
At the place of the tall, brown rock,
At the place under trees where the breeze is,
We go, returning to my earth home.

And Talking God comes with me,
With his long white wand he comes,
Opening a way for me, he comes.
He walks behind me, returning home.
Among the many trails to my home
A way is opened up for me.
In the middle of my broad field,
Beautiful with the white corn,

Beautiful with the yellow corn,
With the pollen from all the corn,
With all kinds of many-colored corn,
The Talking God opens the way for me.

The Home God opens up the way for me.
With his yellow wand he opens the way.
He returns behind me on the way.
The doorway of my house is made of light.
A way is opened to my doorway for me.
By the fireplace in my house,
Through the middle of my house,
Toward the back of my house,
A way is opened up for me.
And Talking God sits down before me,
While Home God sits down behind me.
They sit down with me on the floor of my house,
Where my feet are lying,
Where my legs are lying,
Where my body is lying,
Where my mind is lying,
Where the dust on my feet is lying,
Where my spittle is lying,
Where the hair of my head is lying.

To my feet I have now returned.
To my legs I have now returned.
To my body I have now returned.
To my mind I have now returned.
To the dust of my feet I have returned.
To my spittle I have returned.
To the hair of my head I have returned.

My feet are restored to me.
My legs are restored to me.
My body is restored to me.
My mind is restored to me.
The dust of my feet is restored to me.
My spittle is restored to me.
The hair of my head is restored to me.

The world before me is restored in beauty.
The world behind me is restored in beauty.
The world above me is restored in beauty.
The world below me is restored in beauty.
All things around me are restored in beauty.
My voice is restored in beauty.
It is finished in beauty.
It is finished in beauty.
It is finished in beauty.
It is finished in beauty.

While traveling in his imagination through the lower worlds the medicine man felt that he had become diseased. What this diseased part of himself represented is the occasion for an interesting intuition in Dr. Matthews' writing. He says the old man was aware it was not his visible body or his soul—his "breath of life." Both of these he knew he possessed. Was this other element a kind of spiritual body which the medicine man was conscious of as constituting a part of himself? Could this be the astral body of philosophy or the psyche of modern discussion, Dr. Matthews asks. The old man thought this unknown part belonged not only to his living person but to things that pertained to it such as his saliva, his fallen hair, the dust on his feet, and so on. The Woman Chieftain of Witches could work her spell on the living person if she could come into possession of any of these things.

To restore to the old medicine man this lost element the presence of the principal gods of the Navajo hierarchy is invoked and described. The two young warrior gods have come to the Place of Emergence so that they may go down through it into the lower worlds. They pass through all the necessary dangers and challenge the inevitable guardians in order to reach the hogan of the Woman of Darkness at the center of the lowest world. Here they secure it, the bewitched element, and begin to climb up with it to the earth world. When the old man is reunited with himself in his own world the two young gods are replaced by Talking God and Home God. Dr. Matthews thinks this means that the spiritual or astral man is brought to the home of the corporeal man where the integration takes place, and "all is restored in beauty."

It seems to me this prayer is suggestive of a kind of psychological knowledge which medicine men possess. The various parts of themselves which are projected in imagination as they officiate in the various rites must be called back to themselves or their spiritual energies will be depleted. That they recognize ways of restoring the lost energy, that they know how to integrate their physical and spiritual values through the introversion which prayer represents seems to me to indicate a high degree of human consciousness.

We may conclude that this prayer of a Navajo medicine man shows understanding of the universal motives of the descent of the spirit of man through the dark realms of the lower worlds of the unconscious mind in search of the mysterious lost treasure-substance. This lost element would seem to be any one of a number of things, a child, a jewel, a lover or what is called the soul. Whatever symbol is chosen to stand for the highest value, that is the object of the search. The consequent ascent to the world of light represents the return to wholeness or holiness, to selfhood and completion, "the coming back to himself."

NAVAJO MEDICINE WOMAN

On a clear morning in autumn Lorenzo sent word to me that he was going to deliver a sewing machine to a Navajo matriarch several miles beyond Pinyon. Would I care to go?

I was living that October in the hospitable home of Elizabeth White at Oraibi. This was just the summons for which I had been waiting.

Driving with Lorenzo was an event in itself. If the road was washed out he just drove right over the desert. He had a good car and he trusted the power within it. When he came to sandy places he would step on the gas, and we would shoot through. But anyone who knows the roads, or lack of them, in the Navajo country can imagine some of the adventures through which we lived. We always took oranges, chocolate, sardines and crackers with us, but we generally had to supplement these with Navajo food.

As we sat that morning with our wheels embedded in deep mud

which no shovel or tumbleweed technique could free us from, he told me about his first post at Keam's Canyon. He talked about his father, known as Don Lorenzo, who had established the Hubbell homestead at Ganado. He told me of President Theodore Roosevelt's friendship with Don Lorenzo, how his first act as President of the United States had been to sign the bill returning two hundred acres of Hubbell land which had been included in the new boundaries of the Navajo Reservation.

As we sat there in the warm morning sun he said some Navajo would see us from a distance and come to help us. Soon, over a little rise of land, we heard the traveling song of a Navajo horseman, and there he was with ropes to pull us out.

When we had delivered the sewing machine we found out that a "sing" was going on about a half a mile from there. A medicine woman from Chin Lee was conducting the female part of the Shooting Chant, Lorenzo decided. *Adelante!* And we were there!

Two new hogans in the vastness of the desert earth. Quiet and sun and noonday silence. Evidently it was an early day of the rite for only the family seemed to be around. Lorenzo lifted the blanket and went in the eastern door of the medicine hogan while I waited outside.

I had read that there were no Navajo medicine women, yet I was going to see one in action, I hoped. I heard her singing in a low monotone, and a chorus of male voices joining in. It seemed a long time before Lorenzo came back. I had sent a black abalone shell with him as a present. Then out she came with Lorenzo in an interval of the treatment.

She made an impression on me that is difficult to paint with words. If strength of character and development of individuality are apparent at first glance, I saw them in this extraordinary personality. She seemed to be about fifty-five years of age, of tall, sturdy build, and of immaculate cleanliness. Her serene eyes and air of quiet power pulled me like a magnet into that hogan and kept me watching her as though I had been hypnotized.

Her black velveteen blouse and wide purple skirt made a pleasing complement to her brown skin and black hair. Her hair was streaked with white at the temples and drawn severely back into a large double knot tied with white cord. From her ears long loops of flexible turquoise beads hung, and around her neck were many valuable strings of turquoise, coral and white shell beads. On her hands were silver and turquoise rings and bracelets. Indeed, she looked like the picture of the Queen of Sikkim, the Tibetan Princess, at the Field Museum in Chicago with her similar coral and turquoise jewelry.

I knew that I should sit against the southern wall of the hogan with the women of the family, so I quietly took my place there sitting as the Navajo woman does, on the ground with my legs under me and to one side. Only men could sit with their legs crossed in front of them. I was not to speak or close my eyes during a ceremony. But I could smoke and offer cigarettes to the women around me.

She took the colored sands of the earth, and the wooden weaving batten, the prayer-boards, the medicine in the shells, and molded them all to an inner idea of beauty. From the earth materials she made a pattern she thought satisfying to the gods. She made and remade everything she touched as an artist takes clay and molds it to his hidden idea. She put so much creative power into that hogan that we were all permeated with it.

In the center of the hogan sat two young Navajos, a woman, bare to the waist, with her long, black hair down around her shoulders, and her husband, naked except for a loin cloth, with his hair loose also over his upper body. They sat still, facing the east and Woman Singer. She had led them into the hogan on four yellow foot-steps of pollen, holding on to the other end of her prayer-board. They sat on specially indicated "spirit spots."

After this their child, an albino about four years old, and an old grandmother with a baby in her arms came and sat beside them. It was obvious that the baby was ailing.

Was Woman Singer treating the whole family? Was she purifying the blood stream of it? I never knew. I had heard that among the Hopis it was regarded as a sign of special favor from the gods if an albino child appeared. Perhaps the Navajos did not think so.

To the left of the hogan a chorus of men were sitting. I was told afterward by Lorenzo that the chief assistant to Woman Singer, the one who handled the rattle while she sang and who handed her various articles which she needed, was her son by her first marriage. The older man who led the chorus for her was her present husband.

Taking the prayer-boards one in each hand, she pressed them to the soles of the feet of her patients, singing and praying as she did so. As she intoned the first lines of her song-prayer, the rattle began its rhythm. The chorus gradually got the feel of the lines. One by one they joined in the chant.

Pressing out the evil of disease, massaging the body, she treated each patient upward from the feet, pausing especially below the knees, at the palms of the hands outstretched on the knees, the chest and back between the shoulder blades, the two shoulders, the top of the head, the right and left cheeks and the middle of the mouth. As she worked intently she made long curving gestures with her right hand toward the smoke hole in the center of the ceiling of the hogan. After about forty minutes of this part of the ceremony everyone went out into the sunlight to rest. The two principal patients stood by the medicine woman and lifted their arms to the sun, to draw its power into their bodies. Then they went and sat apart behind the medicine hogan, for they must not touch or speak to anyone while the ceremony was in progress.

Behind them, in the western part of the hogan, I had been looking at two very beautiful small paintings. They were on the floor on big white buckskins, and seemed to be made of very special substances. These were pollen paintings. Instead of colored sands and limestones, corn pollen, ground petals of flowers, turquoise and white shell had been used. They were representations of the sun and the moon, the sun predominantly blue, the moon, white. The sun seemed to be enclosed in a square and the moon in a circle. There were white and yellow lines across the foreheads and chins of these circular faces. In the middle of the faces were long vertical figures, in yellow for the sun and in blue for the moon.

The hours of the afternoon were spent in painting the bodies of the man and his wife. The faces were blackened and the chins painted white. On the arms lightning stripes were painted. But it was on the chests and backs that the intricate work was done. Dipping her colors out of shells beside her, Woman Singer made little figures similar to those on the faces of the sun and moon paintings. Beginning just below the throat she outlined the figure of Pollen

Boy in yellow on the chest of the man and the figure of Cornbug Girl in blue on the woman. She was singing all the time that she did this. The chorus was chanting.

After an hour or so she motioned to the man and woman to turn around and she then painted the backs between the shoulder blades with the reversed symbols. Before they left the hogan she put pinches of pollen from the foot-steps they had walked on into each of their moccasins. They were to continue to walk on the spirit path as they left the hogan.

When the afternoon was over and the patients and chorus had left the hogan, Lorenzo sat beside Woman Singer and talked to her in Navajo. I remained sitting on a pile of sheepskins. After a time he beckoned to me to come over to them, and I sat down beside her. Then she began to show me the things in her medicine bundle as she put them away. There were a number of eagle-feather wands carefully woven together. There were bear claws and snake rattles, a fox skin and a turtle shell. There were many little buckskin bags containing medicine and pollen. There was a set of the little stone figures, one white stone and one grey stone wrapped together with turkey feathers, which are called the Eth-kaynaáshi, the Spirit Bringers. On a flat slab of stone were remnants of turquoise which she had been grinding for the painting. She picked out the largest of these and gave it to me. Then she touched me with several objects and let me hold them in my hands for a moment or two.

When she spoke in Navajo Lorenzo translated. "She wants to know if the woman from California has seen the western islands off the coast." She meant the islands off the coast at Santa Barbara, so I nodded that I had. These islands are thought to be the home of the Turquoise Woman, so I knew why she was interested. "She says the woman from California may come to see any of her ceremonies. She wants to know if you can get her any more of the black abalone shells. She says the wisdom of the snake, and strength of the bear, the swiftness of the eagle, and the cunning of the fox will help you on your journey."

I saw her once more, some years after this ceremony, when she came to Lorenzo's post. She had come to beg Lorenzo, as some medicine men had done, to let her give a particular ceremony over him. He was very ill with heart and kidney trouble. He sat there wrapped up by his fire, and she sat there beside him for about two hours. At the end of the afternoon she bent over him, took his hand and held it, looking into his eyes, saying never a word. Then she left. He said the next morning that he had slept well that night, that she had done him more good than all the medicine which was coming up from Winslow.

NAVAJO SAND PAINTINGS

The first sand painting which I saw was on the fifth evening of a Night Chant. It seemed to be a circular design of gods kneeling on the four ends of a large black cross. The ends of the cross were of equal length, reaching in the four directions from a small black central circle which was surrounded by four lines of soft colors. Between the arms of the cross were long corn plants with their roots emanating from the center. The whole arrangement was almost completely enclosed by the long figure of a rainbow goddess with her square head at one end and her little skirt and feet at the other. It was called the Whirling Logs Sand Painting.

The figures of the gods were intricately drawn. They had been abstractly conceived in long rectangles, circles, squares and triangles. I had seen much "modern art" in galleries in Europe and America, but I had never seen anything so provocative of inner reaction, so exciting to the imagination, as this picture made of dry sands and charcoal and ground stone. The entire floor of the medicine hogan, about fifteen feet across, was filled by this circular painting. There was just enough room left around the walls for the medicine man, his helpers and a few onlookers to seat themselves.

Lorenzo and I had been waiting to see the prayer-sticks and bull-roarer taken into the medicine lodge. These and a number of other objects from the bundle of the Chanter had been deposited outside the hogan on a mound of sand in the early morning. They constituted the sign that a sand painting was being made within. We had entered and taken our proper places as these important properties were being disposed around the painting in their ceremonial positions.

Then, for just a few minutes, a Navajo sand painting existed before our eyes in its subtle and convincing artistry—ephemeral loveliness inside a darkish hut of mud and logs. But even as we stared, long black lines of charcoal were strewn over the entire surface. Tiny mounds of pollen and corn meal were deposited at various points on the painting. The patient was seated in the middle of it, and the exquisite symmetry of the figures was being destroyed. This was inevitable. I tried to hold the delicate beauty of the painting in my memory.

I knew that the sand paintings were made from the time of sunrise through the middle of the day by the Chanter and his assistants, and that they were destroyed in the late afternoon. The Navajos believed that the gods had first shown their patterns to certain heroic men on the clouds or on sacred buckskins. They knew that the power of the divine designs was too great to remain in the permanent possession of the earth people, so they decreed that no reproductions were to be made. The knowledge of the paintings was handed down only in the memories of the initiated medicine men. And they were to be used ritually and destroyed in a prescribed manner.

Lorenzo said the black lines of charcoal represented the divine waves of power and were the final consecration of the painting. All sand paintings were "tied in," he said—that is, they were surrounded and protected by the Rainbow Goddess, or by an elongated snake, or by strings of lightning. These outer lines were circular or square or rectangular in form. They were open to the east, the direction of least evil, and two little figures of harvest flies, weasels or other animals guarded the opening. The power of the paintings was too strong to be allowed to emanate outwardly. This power must be held in for use in the curing of the patient.

Circles were not supposed to be closed by living human beings. A closed circle meant something finished, and that might mean death. Moreover, there had to be a doorway for the entrance and exit of the spirits of the gods, and if any evil got into a painting, it had to have an exit left for it.

I tried to see as many sand paintings as I could. One day I took a friend to see one. All that she could say afterward was, "What wonderful imaginations the Navajos have!" But I had thought that, too, and was not satisfied with it as a summation. I looked up "imagination" in the dictionary, and the gist of what it said was, "the power of making images." When I looked up "images" they seemed to be defined as pictures produced inwardly by the brain of a man. I left my slowly forming conclusions to further experience.

I began to make a collection of sand paintings. I learned to memorize them as I sat in the medicine hogans. When you have seen a number of them you can begin to do that. You note the known details of the new one. You can say to yourself, "Center, black with four sun-rafts, sacred plants as usual, four gods of the various directions, four buffalo in between, rainbow tying picture in usual form." If the picture is unusual in any way, you concentrate on the new elements. In an interval of the making of them you sit outside the hogan and fix all the parts in your mental picture. When you go back inside again you go over that inner picture and correct it or complete it. I made my paintings on heavy tan paper about twenty-eight by twenty-two inches in size as soon as I could get back to my materials.

There seemed to be an endless number of them. There are probably five or six hundred different paintings belonging to the various myth systems. Some of them repeat the same motifs over and over but always in a slightly different way. By the time that I had copied thirty or forty I knew something of the "magic" of their influence. Each one represented a centralizing or integrating experience.

The "palette" of the medicine man as he works on or directs a painting is a limited one, but it represents a very pleasing range of color. Held by necessity to the use of dry materials, he has to use the colors of the rocks and earth around him. After the floor of the medicine hogan has been spread with clean, new sand, spread evenly by the weaving battens of the women, the colors are ground very carefully by the medicine man and his assistants. Perhaps he has some special color in one of the little buckskin bags of his medicine bundle. On pieces of bark and in shells, the ground colors lie around him as he works crouched in the center of the new sand. The paintings are all made from the center outward, of course. In making the figures in the four directions the work proceeds from right to left as the hands of a clock travel. The beginning point is in the east when there is no specific center.

Pieces of yellow and red limestone have been pounded and ground for the yellows and reds and rose colors of the paintings. Wood specially charred has furnished the soft grey-black; mixed with white sand it also makes the grey-blue, so necessary to the paintings. Earth from special locations has provided the red-brown used for the heads of the gods. Powdered turquoise and azurite and malachite are sometimes used, and there are paintings in which corn meal and pollen and ground flower petals are used.

All these are muted colors, soft and subtle shadings. There is none of the so-called "primitive" coloring—no violent oranges and crimsons.

Four colors are used over and over again. These are the ceremonial colors of the four directions of the earth. White is generally in the east, blue in the south, yellow in the west, and black in the north. They are used in that order, also, clockwise—although I have heard that in some paintings used in witchcraft rituals, these colors are laid on in the reversed direction. Black and white are sometimes interchangeable. White is used at times in the north and black in the east. When this is done it is said the painting usually presents a situation which happened in one of the former worlds. Black and yellow are said to be masculine colors, and blue and white feminine ones, but I have seen them used in opposite connotations. Objects which are white are surrounded with black lines and vice versa. Those which are blue or yellow are outlined in the opposite color. This is to suggest a harmony in the inclusion of the contrasting male and female colors.

A soft pink, called the sparkling color because it is usually sprinkled with mica, is used in the representation of certain medicinal herbs, in the making of mirages or for thunder divinities. A rich red-brown or henna color covers the heads of the gods and goddesses. A dark red is used in the rainbow and sun-rafts. Add to these a blue-green which is used for the small details of the spruce and fir boughs, and we have the simple color scheme of the sand paintings. Turquoise and other blues may be added if these are necessary.

The Chanter squats on his heels as he works. His right hand reaches out to a shell filled with powdered color or to a mound of colored sand on a piece of bark or buckskin. Holding the colored sand in the cupped palm of his hand he lets it trickle out over his curved forefinger, guiding the little stream with his thumb. He has allocated certain parts of the painting to various assistants whom he watches carefully as they work. The pattern for the picture exists only in his mind but certain of his helpers have worked with him so often that they can be trusted. The only part in which these men may be allowed to improvise is on the tobacco pouches and skirts of the gods. They vie with each other in making beautiful designs as they come to these places.

The men smoke and joke with each other as they work. At intervals they go out and sit in the sun. At other times they are engaged in eating the good food the women of the patient's family are sending in to them. They know each other well. Many of the most skilled sand artists follow the winter "sings" around for the sake of practicing their art and to participate in the good cheer of the ceremonies.

In the early afternoon the patient is led in by the Chanter and seated in the middle of the painting. As the Chanter sings the prayers and the chorus joins in, he rubs sand from each part of the figures of the gods on the corresponding parts of the patient's body. There is much massage of the body at this time. There is also much whistling and blowing away of the spirits of the disease. The eagle-feather wands, the prayer-boards and the gourd rattle are in use.

The Chanter rubs out each figure as he uses it. He uses the sands of the figures from the center outward as he applies them to the patient. After he is through, the sand is gathered up in blankets and taken to the north where it is deposited hastily under a tree. It is thought that the illness might reside in the sands. Had not the body of the patient become progressively stronger and sounder as the painting was destroyed?

If you want to see a sand painting it is best to engage the kindly offices of a trader on the reservation. Since most of them are interested enough to know when a "sing" is going to take place, they can obtain the consent of the medicine man for the entrance of a well-disposed stranger into the medicine hogan. An appropriate present of tobacco or abalone shells and proper silent behavior while viewing the making of the picture would ensure this privilege.

If you become interested in sand paintings you cannot help

being drawn into the discussions which go on about their origins. Various anthropologists dismiss them as being borrowed in "acculturation patterns" from other tribes. But it seems to me this theory does not account for the great development of them among the Navajos. Of course, The People probably saw the wall paintings in the kivas of the older Pueblo villages on their arrival in Arizona and New Mexico. They also must have seen the sand altars of the Hopis and Zuñis. One can recognize in the reproductions of the murals of Awátobi and Kua-húa-hua today slight resemblances to the figures in the Navajo sand paintings. The same elongated bodies and triangulated skirt forms are there, and certain small conventionalized cloud forms. But how much more apparent are the differences than the resemblances! In most of the reproductions of the Kua-húa-hua murals which I have seen there is little, if any, organization of design. The conventionalization of the Awátobi designs is of a different nature from that of the Navajo conceptions. In none of them is there the harmonious use of the designed symbols in the great variety and skillful repetition of the Navajo paintings, or the intricate exactitude of detail.

Of course, other American Indian tribes have made sand paintings. I have seen a copy of one which the Papagos make today, a circular arrangement of animals representing the months of the year. I have seen copies of the sand altars of the Zuñis. To claim a specific tribal origin for the art of sand painting has little to do with the question. Various tribes made baskets because they needed them in their economies. They wove when they found the wild cotton. In the same way they made sand paintings when they had to have a means of depicting the principles of their religions.

The reproduction of the sand painting at the beginning of this book is from the Blessing Chant. This is a short ceremony which may be incorporated in longer rites and may be given at any time of the year. Parts of it may be given on one day and all of it on five days. It contains no exorcistic practices as on the first four days of the nine-day chantways. The painting is smaller and less complicated than the majority of the big paintings. In it the patient, or initiate, enters on the red and blue path at the lower right on four spirit foot-steps of cornmeal, then proceeds on the yellow pollen path between the upraised arms of the mysterious

Ethkaynaáshi, or Spirit Bringers. This path leads him into the white field of ritual ceremony by the Navajo Tree of Life, the Great Corn Plant. He has to pass through both female and male experience as he moves upward, the female part being symbolized by the smooth, curved lines of the rainbow and the male by the crooked, dynamic lines of the lightning. Passing out at the top of the painting through the corn tassels he comes to the Blue Bird, which signifies blessing and peace, and goes out into the world again on the yellow pollen path at the upper right.

If one wishes to see the most developed of the Navajo sand paintings, there are excellent reproductions in Professor Reichard's *Sand Paintings of the Navajo Shooting Chant* and *Navajo Medicine Man*, books which have been out of print for a long time. The Museum of Navajo Ceremonial Art at Santa Fe, New Mexico, has a large collection of copies of sand paintings, and Miss Wheelwright has published some of these in her books on *The Creation Myth* and *The Hail and Water Chants*. Mr. A. M. Stephen and Dr. Washington Matthews have a few sand paintings in their books and articles on the Night Chant and the Mountain Chant. In my book *Beautiful on the Earth*, which is now out of print, I have four of the large sand paintings and their descriptions, as well as a reproduction of the little known Sun House screen. But these illustrations of the myths are very difficult and expensive to reproduce. We must be content to know a few of these sand paintings, which form one of the most differentiated and imaginative design systems that primitive man has ever originated.

BIBLIOGRAPHY

COOLIDGE, DANE, AND MARY ROBERTS. *The Navajo Indians.* Boston: Houghton Mifflin Co., 1930.

FEWKES, WALTER J. "Hindu and Parsee Sand Painting," *The Archeologist.* Vol. 3, No. 1, January 1895.

GILLMOR, FRANCES, AND LOUISA WADE WETHERILL. *Traders to the Navajo.* Boston: Houghton Mifflin Co., 1934.

GODDARD, PLINY EARLE. *Indians of the Southwest.* New York: American Museum of Natural History, 1931.

Navajo Texts. New York: American Museum of Natural History, 1933.

HAILE, FATHER BERARD. *Origin Legend of the Navaho Enemy Way.* New Haven: Yale University Press, 1938.

"Navajo Chantways and Ceremonials," *American Anthropologist,* Vol. 40, No. 4, 1938.

An Ethnologic Dictionary of the Navaho Language. Saint Michaels, Arizona: Press of the Franciscan Fathers, 1910.

HILL, W. W. *The Agricultural and Hunting Methods of the Navaho Indians.* New Haven: Yale University Press, 1938.

HODGE, FREDERICK WEBB. "The Early Navajo and Apache," *American Anthropologist,* Vol. 8, No. 3, 1895.

JENNESS, DIAMOND. "Prehistoric Culture Waves from Asia to America," *Annual Report,* Smithsonian Institute, 1941.

JUNG, CARL G. *Psychology and Religion.* New Haven: Yale University Press, 1938.

JUNG, CARL G., AND RICHARD WILHELM. *The Secret of the Golden Flower.* London: Kegan, Paul, Trench Co., 1931.

KLUCKHOHN, CLYDE, AND LELAND WYMAN. "An Introduction to Navaho Chant Practice," *American Anthropologist*, Vol. 42, Supp. No. 53, 1940.

LINCOLN, J. S. *The Dream in Primitive Cultures*. Baltimore: The Williams & Wilkins Company, 1935.

MALINOWSKI, BRONISLAW. *Myth in Primitive Psychology*. New York: W. W. Norton & Company, Inc., 1927.

MATTHEWS, WASHINGTON. *The Night Chant*. New York: American Museum of Natural History, 1902.

"Songs of Sequence of the Navajos," *Journal of American Folk Lore*, Vol. 7, No. 26, 1894.

"A Vigil of the Gods. A Navajo Ceremony," *American Anthropologist*, Vol 9, No. 2, 1896.

"The Origin of the Utes. A Navajo Myth." *American Antiquarian*, Vol. 7, No. 5, 1885.

"A Night with the Navajos," *Forest and Stream*, Vol. 23, 1884.

"Navajo Gambling Songs," *American Anthropologist*, Vol. 2, No. 1, 1889.

"The Prayer of a Navajo Shaman," *American Anthropologist*, Vol. 1, No. 2, 1888.

"Some Deities and Demons of the Navajos," *American Naturalist*, Vol. 20, 1886.

Mountain Chant. Report Bureau of Ethnology, Vol. 5, 1883–84.

Navaho Legends. New York: G. E. Stechert and Co., 1897.

"Songs of the Navajos," *Land of Sunshine*, Los Angeles, 1896.

"Mythic Dry Paintings of the Navajos," *American Naturalist*, Vol. 19, No. 10.

MORGAN, WILLIAM. "Navajo Dreams," *American Anthropologist*, Vol. 34, No. 3, 1932.

NEWCOMB, FRANC JOHNSON. *Navajo Omens and Taboos*. Santa Fe: Rydal Press, 1940.

REICHARD, GLADYS A., AND FRANC JOHNSON NEWCOMB. *Sandpaintings of the Navajo Shooting Chant*. New York: J. J. Augustin Co., 1937.

Navajo Shepherd and Weaver. New York: J. J. Augustin Co., 1936.

Prayer: The Compulsive Word. New York: Monographs of the American Ethnological Society, 1944.

SAPIR, EDWARD. "A Navajo Sand Painting Blanket," *American Anthropologist*, Vol. 37, 1935.

SCHEVILL, MARGARET ERWIN. *Beautiful on the Earth*. Santa Fe: Hazel Dreis Editions, 1947.

SPINDEN, HERBERT JOSEPH. *Songs of the Tewa*. New York: Exposition of Indian Tribal Arts, 1933.

STEPHEN, A. M. "The Navajo," *American Anthropologist*, Vol. 6, No. 4, 1893.

"Navajo Origin Legend," *Journal of American Folk Lore*, Vol. 43, No. 167, 1930.

WALTON, EDA LOU. "Navajo Song Patterning," *Journal of American Folk Lore*, Vol. 43, No. 167, 1930.

WHEELWRIGHT, MARY CABOT. *Navajo Creation Myth*. Santa Fe: Rydal Press, 1942.

Hail Chant and Water Chant. Santa Fe: Museum of Navajo Ceremonial Art, 1946.

WYMAN, LELAND C. "The Female Shooting Life Chant," *American Anthropologist*, Vol. 38, 1936.

INDEX